VOLUME 1: Perseverance

CULTURE OF REVIVAL

a revivalist field manual

Jeremy Bardwell - Brian Brennt - Jake Hamilton
Jason Hershey - Rick Pino - Amy Sollars - Taylor Stutts

ANDY BYRD - SEAN FEUCHT

Culture of Revival: A Revivalist Field Manual
Volume 1: Perseverance with Joy

Cover design by Jeremy Bardwell
Interior design by David Sluka

Published by Fire and Fragrance
Paperback ISBN: 978-0-9854955-0-3
Ebook ISBN: 978-0-9854955-1-0

www.fireandfragrance.com
www.thecircuitrider.com
www.burn24-7.com

Printed in the United States of America for Worldwide Distribution

Endorsements

THIS BOOK IS FILLED WITH INSIGHTS to equip the reader for a lifestyle of sustained revival. The authors are all torchbearers for this great move of God, yet their instruction is profoundly practical, paving the way for a generation to complete the mandate given by God. Read as one who has no options but to please God with every breath, and you, too, will burn with a holy fire!

Bill Johnson
Bethel Church – Redding, CA
Author, *When Heaven Invades Earth* and
Essential Guide to Healing

CULTURE OF REVIVAL IS A CRUCIAL MESSAGE to bring revelation for what a cultural reformation will look like in this current global wave of God. Sean Feucht and Andy Byrd are burgeoning young leaders, full of godly character and fresh articulation, calling a generation into abandonment and total obedience to Jesus and His teachings.

Mike Bickle
International House of Prayer – Kansas City, MO
Author, *Passion For Jesus* and *After God's Own Heart*

I LOVE THESE GUYS! My heart is so deeply moved to see this new breed of young men and women who love and honor their spiritual fathers and who carry a double portion of their love, their anointing, their vision, and their sacrifice.

When I read this book, hope erupts in me like never before with expectation for a glorious revival manifestation and an earth-shaking cultural transformation. Jesus, ruin every reader with a vision for this kind of Christianity to fill the earth!

Lou Engle
www.thecall.com

SEAN FEUCHT AND ANDY BYRD are "burning men" lighting up the nations with fire for revival. They are incredible leaders, filled with passion to see a move of God in the earth. Before we knew them personally, we saw them coming. Years ago, in the midst of a global renewal we were part of, God began to speak of an even greater revival to come—a revival in the next generation. We have prayed for years to see this generation arise. Now they are here.

In this awesome book, Sean and Andy have gathered others who are paving the way to see a "generation that will change society and society will not change them." *Culture of Revival* will show you the fire that is already burning and prepare you to become part of a generation on fire for revival.

Wesley and Stacey Campbell
www.revivalnow.com and www.beahero.org

SEAN FEUCHT IS SUCH AN EXAMPLE of a wholly-given, radical lover of God! He has a contagious passion for the Lord that draws people closer to the Father's heart and deeper into His presence. When I first encountered Fire and Fragrance, I knew it was my tribe. Worshipping with these young people who are completely given to the Lord encouraged me into an even deeper place in God. Sean is simply a delight!

Heidi Baker, PhD
Founding Director, Iris Global

WHEN I FIRST MET SEAN AND ANDY, I was profoundly affected by their passion and purity. In the years since, I've watched their influence and impact grow exponentially. They carry a fiery, holy love across the earth, feeding the culture of that which sustains revival.

The pages of this book are incendiary and dripping with oil from the lives of some of the great, young revivalists alive today. Read it with an open heart and you just might be set on fire and launched into a life of unending love!

Charles Stock
Senior Leader, Life Center Ministries
Harrisburg, Pennsylvania

Dedication

To the Fathers and Mothers
who have gone before us to to pave the way for this culture of revival to emerge. We honor the sacrifices, obedience, and suffering you have embraced to see God's kingdom come! You have truly taught us perseverance with joy!

Contents

The Call

Preface

�֍

We hear a lot of talk about revival, and we think there should be even more. Revival is birthed in the heart of God and transferred to anyone who has faith for the impossible.

Through *Culture of Revival*, we want to articulate some of the teachings, cultural components, and practical understandings about revival. The goal of revival is not evening meetings and big conferences, although these may very well result. But ultimately, revival must touch the very fabric of society. It must move beyond an individual to the family, to the neighborhood, to the Church, and flow into the nations.

When John Wesley first visited Herrnhut, Germany, to see the Moravian movement, his response was, "When will this Christianity fill the earth?" What he encountered was more than a man named Zinzendorf, more than a vibrant church, and more than a place of prayer and hard work. He experienced a revival culture that had so inundated the Moravian people that for the first time in his life he understood what the kingdom of heaven could look like on earth.

This is the first volume of a series. Other books to come will highlight different aspects of this culture and draw from diverse voices across the body of Christ. We have much to learn from each other. In a spirit of meekness and humility, we will see the gospel of the kingdom grip the heart of a generation. We want to see regional revivals become a global great awakening preparing the way for the return of our King.

In this book, *Volume One: Perseverance with Joy,* we will highlight various aspects of overcoming, perseverance, intimacy, and sustainability. Read, act, and change the world!

Andy Byrd and Sean Feucht

The Call

❖

INTRODUCTION

The Anthem of the Three Hundred

By Brian Brennt

The against-all-odds story of Gideon has inspired generations since God used three hundred men to defeat over one hundred twenty thousand trained soldiers. It was an amazing victory, and it started with *discontentment*.

> When the angel of the LORD appeared to Gideon, he said, "The LORD is with you, mighty warrior."
>
> "Pardon me, my lord," Gideon replied, "but if the LORD is with us, why has all this happened to us? Where are all his wonders that our ancestors told us about when they said, 'Did not the LORD bring us

up out of Egypt?' But now the LORD has abandoned us and given us into the hand of Midian."

—Judges 6:12-13

Can you feel the frustration, the bewilderment, the discontentment in Gideon's voice? Today there is a similar stirring. If you listen, you can hear a new sound rumbling. It is the sound of a Jesus Revolution rolling in like a wave far out at sea. The wave is barely detectable to the human eye, but the hearts of this generation can feel its arrival. This is not a business-as-usual hour, but rather an hour of historic importance.

At the root of the discontent, cynicism, and disillusionment is an intuitive sense that something is about to change. The wilderness of your preparation is not a place to make your camp. It is now time to cross over. Like an old car that you know will never make the journey, you are getting out knowing it would be safer to walk than debate what does or does not work.

Dear brave one, arise, for you have been hardwired to drive the new sound—Jesus awaits you! Like a storm that is sure to come, the old roof is not going to stand. If you run after Jesus now, you can make it to safety. Get up and run now. Jesus is calling you to Himself and He is not distant. You are scheduled for a visitation and your name is written on His hand. He has been waiting for this moment. He is guiding you through the storm to the promise.

Jesus is calling you, and with this call you'll need to be brave. Bravery is going up against the odds like the three hundred did. Or maybe that's just insanity. How can you win a battle—or start a revival—with only three hundred? Gideon's army didn't start with three hundred. He started with thirty-two thousand. But then God said to him,

> "You have too many men. I cannot deliver Midian into their hands, or Israel would boast against me, 'My own strength has saved me.'" —Judges 7:2

The army dropped twenty-two thousand to ten thousand, but that was still too many. So the Lord provided a test to narrow down the field once again. With that three hundred, God saved Israel from their enemies.

Gideon's three hundred experienced an encounter with the living God. It is a story of ordinary turned into extraordinary. It is a story of decisions made in great difficulty that won the day and turned the worst of times into the greatest of times.

God will always choose weakness to display His strength and power. This army saw what God had done in previous generations. That's why Gideon was so discontent. But when it came to the battle, they had a choice to make: human ingenuity, strategy, and methods or a humble road with an entry door so low that they had to get on their faces to pass through it.

You cannot see this door unless you are broken—gladly and willingly. Once they saw this door, their weaknesses were displayed before their very eyes. They witnessed the impossibility of bravery in their faces, yet Jesus pulled them through. His hand was reaching to them through the low door that He had chosen for Himself. He delighted in their position. He could not withhold His response; He reached for them.

He is there at the door now, reaching once again for those who do not feel brave or up to the task of this hour. Jesus cannot contain Himself as He reaches out. Don't you feel His hand pulling you into this hour? A most severe surrender is in your heart to offer Jesus. Your sacrifice will be expensive, but there is no other choice. You feel His hand in yours and the unordinary calls to you. That is how the three hundred felt in their day.

✳ Bravery and severe sacrifice always shifts history. In generation after generation, when Jesus is getting ready to turn the hour, He searches for a person to move through—someone who will be eager to offer a severe sacrifice. However, first you must see Him, for then you will only remember His sacrifice and not your own.

Gideon's story is about a young man who could not hear the sound of a visitation and a coming victory. The roars of the dark armies of his day were so loud that he hid. This is a story of hard decisions and separation and of raw courage that led to the heights of incredible triumph. In the end, this is a story of an encounter that led to a sound that broke the darkness.

> The Israelites did evil in the eyes of the LORD, and for seven years he gave them into the hands of the Midianites. Because the power of Midian was so oppressive, the Israelites prepared shelters for themselves in mountain clefts, caves and strongholds. Whenever the Israelites planted their crops, the Midianites, Amalekites and other eastern peoples invaded the country. They camped on the land and ruined the crops all the way to Gaza and did not spare a living thing for Israel, neither sheep nor cattle nor donkeys. They came up with their livestock and

their tents like swarms of locusts. It was impossible to count them or their camels; they invaded the land to ravage it. Midian so impoverished the Israelites that they cried out to the LORD for help.

—Judges 6:1-6

Gideon and the three hundred were raised up under great oppression. Every year the harvest was ruined before their eyes. They plowed, planted, and worked for harvest. They toiled in the sweat and anxiety of sowing, always knowing that last season all they had worked for had been taken from them. Theft was so rampant that not a sheep, cattle, or donkey was spared. The enemy was so overpowering that their numbers were described like a swarm of locusts. They dreamed, but all of their dreams were about the great deliverances and miracles of years long ago.

Because the power of Midian was so oppressive, the Israelites prepared shelters for themselves in mountain clefts, caves, and strongholds. This domination overpowered the bravery in their hearts as they were driven to live outside of the places of their inheritance. The silence of bravery became the norm and with it came the cruelty of dreams being shelved. The people were driven from the places of fulfillment and they hid, hoping only to be left alone. In their hiding, they gave themselves to pursuing answers from gods they built with their hands and sinful desires. They were drenched in every form of darkness and they lost their sight—forgetting the One who held victory in His hands.

To be sure, the Midianites were not there uninvited. Their oppression was directly connected to the sin of Israel.

The Israelites did evil in the eyes of the Lord, and
for seven years he gave them into the hands of the
Midianites. —Judges 6:1

Here we read about a nation who continually gave themselves over to sin, and with that lifestyle came great oppression.
It is an amazing commentary on the human heart that is so quick
to forget the ramifications of national sin. Israel was not new to
this cycle, yet it took year after year of violent oppression for the
nation to cry out to God.

It is worth noting that they did indeed cry out to God and
the answer to their cry was a prophet. Deliverance was indeed
already scheduled, but first the nation had to understand the root
of the oppression. We are not told who this prophet was, nor
where he came from, but his message was clear. The message
from God was:

"I brought you up out of Egypt, out of the land of
slavery. I rescued you from the hand of the Egyptians.
And I delivered you from the hand of all your
oppressors; I drove them out before you and gave you
their land. I said to you, 'I am the Lord your God; do
not worship the gods of the Amorites, in whose land
you live.' But you have not listened to me."

—Judges 6:8-10

The prophet explained the situation, leaving Israel with no
confusion as to what was happening in the nation. We are not
told if any of the three hundred were there that day listening to
the prophet, nor are we told if the message spread to all of Israel.

From Gideon's response, it would seem that the message had not reached all of Israel.

Sin brings oppression, followed by a cry for relief. The cry is met with grace and mercy. Knowing why you are oppressed, or even that you are oppressed, is nothing short of grace and mercy. The drastic in-your-face oppression Israel experienced had its advantages. There was no confusion or spin that could be put on it. The oppression was out in the open, and they experienced the result of it every day. Midian was not having a *gradual* effect on Israel, nor did the people of Israel disagree on what was being stolen from them. The oppression was clear, and it resulted in a unified cry for freedom.

The three hundred had story after story of what was stolen from them, their families, and their cities. There were not twenty-five different opinions as to what the cause of their misery was. Midian was the reason, and so the prophet told them the root cause. Idolatry had brought them into this misery and only God could bring them out.

Had the prophet told them that their deliverance would come from three hundred of their own countrymen, or that the very least among them would lead one of the most daring military operations to be remembered for thousands of years, they would never have believed it. The prophet brought the reason, but God Himself would bring the deliverance—and it would start with God choosing a deliverer.

For us now, the oppression of Midian takes a much different approach. We are not so much under a sudden and drastic oppression as much as continual, gradual assaults that have the very same end. Oppression is about total domination and it involves open cruelty. This is what Israel faced day in and day out for seven years. They lived under military occupation and the daily oppression was both systematic and complete.

In America today, Christianity is not so much under a brutal occupation by the enemy, but it is under a more sophisticated assault. The assault gradually rises almost imperceptibly on a daily basis. You cannot remember the exact day that the culture changed. The assault on Jesus carries on each year and we have come to a critical juncture.

Today, Christians do not react with the same indignation and rage as Israel did in the day of Midian because of the gradual rate of being converted and conformed to secularism. The Jesus of the gospels and the culture He promoted is being replaced with secular humanism. The pure gospel and nothing but the pure gospel is the only way back.

All across this nation, untapped bravery is about to step onto the stage of history. The assault has been overwhelming and intimidating, but when it is broken down into simplicity, all confusion clears and the way is straightforward.

You may be facing impossible illness. You may be lying in a hospital bed wondering if you will ever go home. You may be sitting in your college dorm watching the setting of the old dreams of America. Maybe you are working a job that has not captured your heart, or debt has captured your future.

You have a voice, but right now no one is listening. You have a song, but it is ahead of its time. You wonder if the words will ever be heard. You could be commuting so much right now, running between college and work, that exhaustion has already found you at a young age. There are sorrows of lost years where relationships stole more from you than anyone could ever understand.

You cannot know the triumph that is before you without touching tragedy. The three hundred must have felt like you do. Yet somewhere in their hearts, they cried out for a day where that victory deep within them would live.

This book is a compilation of chapters from young Gideons who have stared at the same impossibilities that Gideon did. They, like yourself, have been in a season of preparation, and with this preparation have come messages. These messages are like trumpet blasts alerting all of our hearts that this is the hour for the gospel to once again arise in every heart. They are some of the messages that are preparing the Gideons of this hour. They are the young voices erupting with new passion and vision for the sound of the gospel to be unleashed.

This book is a book of impartation. It is written for the Father to press the courage of Jesus into your heart. An impartation happens when you receive something beyond an education. It is caught not taught. An impartation is more than you being inspired or motivated; it happens when you are transformed and begin to live out the very things you learned. Through this book, we desire you to receive the miraculous. Arise from where ever you are in this moment, and take a hold of your critical place. For without your voice, the sound cannot fully break forth into this coming Jesus movement.

Your story is the story of Gideon and the three hundred. It is a call to follow Jesus. Receive an impartation of courage, initiative, and ultimately, revolution. But first, encounter the only true revolutionary—His name is Jesus. Gideon: it is your hour and the time for training is now. May this be an anthem of training in your heart.

ABOUT THE AUTHOR: Brian Brennt and his wife, Christy, have a call of God on their lives to awaken, prepare, and see revival break out in America and ripple across the world. They are passionate soul winners who carry the message of the gospel everywhere they go. They are firmly believing God for the mobilization of a massive wave of missionaries out of America. Forged through the place of intercession and brokenness, their entire family carries the same burden for revival. Brian is a graduate of Faith Seminary where he earned a Doctorate in Leadership. The beginning days of Brian and Christy's ministry came out of an outbreak of salvation and repentance in Tacoma, Washington. They function often as a team and are filled with the joy that can only come from spending time together in the place of prayer. Their children are Nick (20), Chloe (18), Spencer (16), and Joshua (10). To contact Brian and Christy, or to order their books (*The Freedom Manual, Big 10 – Truth Encounters,* and *Salvation Encounter*), e-mail them at salvationencounter@gmail.com.

The Culture

✵

✳❖

ONE

Culture Revolution

By Andy Byrd

On July 7, 2010, the Lord powerfully visited our Youth With a Mission Fire and Fragrance community in Kona, Hawaii. Amy Sollars, one of our leaders and a contributing author in this book, was praying for revelation when she experienced the following. Below is a brief excerpt of what happened during that encounter:

> As I waited on the Lord, I was given an encounter and message from the Lord where I saw a heavenly messenger dressed in clothes like those worn during the colonial period in America. In my spirit, I knew he looked like Paul Revere. He had a messenger bag and he said that he represented a people that would bring a message. "They will 'ride' through the night to declare and prepare the

27

way for a revolution that will lead to reformation."
He said that in the bag were documents related to this
and were about the release of glory. He said that there
were people who were to go and sound an alarm—an
awakening alarm.

As a community, we have a value and culture that no revelation supersedes or contradicts the truths revealed in Scripture. At the same time, we pay attention when God speaks in these ways.

In response to this encounter, we went into a season of waiting on God for confirmation of this vision and revelation of what it meant. The encounter seemed fairly explanatory in itself: God is raising up a generation that will be like Paul Revere, carrying an urgent message that will lead to revolution and ultimately reformation. However, this is not a political or violent revolution, but rather an overthrow of all spiritual darkness that reigns in our lives and in our communities. From this message of revolution, many would be awakened to the truth and Lordship of Jesus. The reformation that would follow would be a cultural reformation. It would not be ethnic culture as in the Korean culture or the Norwegian culture, but a culture that both transcends and enriches human cultures.

Amy's description of the encounter continued:

Next he said that the Lord was releasing "circuit riders"
again. I saw these different circuits and this wild-eyed
revivalist declaring the gospel. I saw these lines of fire
igniting wherever they rode.

We understood this to mean that God will release revolution messengers who will carry the message of the simple gospel to the highways and byways of the nation. They will go preaching the love of God; total and absolute surrender to his Lordship; and joy-filled, cross-bearing obedience. Their very lives will be based on the truth of the Bible and the teachings on the life of Jesus. These messengers will be cultural warriors whose very presence, power, and lifestyle will provoke the Bride to step into its promised glory and the lost to accept their Savior! A major move of God becomes possible with messengers like this—people who will truly live for Christ, or die for gain. Persecution, setbacks, and disappointments are unable to stop a generation like this.

The world has seen a generation like this before. During the late 1700s and the early 1800s, the circuit riders were a mobile band of selfless and radical preachers and teachers. Much of the westward expansion of the gospel, as well as the carrying out of the simple gospel message and the transformational power released through the Second Great Awakening, can be attributed to them. In fact, they helped to establish a national culture in their day.

Their work contributed to the paving of a Biblical worldview as a major part of the foundation of our nation. Their lives made the Second Great Awakening possible! Then, they took that message from the camp meetings of the South to remote homes everywhere. During this period, hundreds of thousands of people began to follow Jesus!

Their early culture was established by men of great spiritual hunger and deep brokenness for the lost such as John Wesley and Francis Asbury. When Asbury first arrived on the shores of America in 1771, there were a few hundred Methodists and a few dozen Methodist preachers. By the time he died in 1816, there were over 210,000 Methodists and over 4,000 preachers. Many of these were circuit-riding preachers. The culture of Asbury's life was radical, selfless, and sacrificial. He was dedicated to the Word of God. He was broken for the lost and he drew his vitality from deep intimacy with God.

This became the culture modeled by the circuit riders everywhere they rode. Half of them died before age thirty-three from sickness, attack, and hard, physical conditions. Yet they kept riding and the gospel kept moving forward.

When one young rider asked Asbury what his pay would be if he became a circuit rider, Asbury replied by saying, "Grace here and glory hereafter... if you are faithful." These men knew they were signing up for martyrdom, very few earthly rewards, and for most of them, a life of celibacy. Yet they considered it a great honor to be a circuit rider. Few aspired to it, and those who did were sometimes hated and sometimes loved.

They were unrelenting in hope and determination to see America bless God, so that God might bless America. One young rider, Jesse Lewis, was commissioned to St. Louis. Upon arriving, he declared, "I have come in the name of Jesus Christ to take St. Louis, and by the grace of God I will do it!" This kind of child-like faith marked the riders and was imparted into a fledgling nation that would need faith for many coming hardships.

Much of the culture of the riders was based on a simple love for Jesus, a radical life of holiness, a deep love for people, and a belief that simple obedience could change history. Themes of abiding and obeying mark the circuit riders from beginning to end. The circuit riders loved these quotes from Asbury.[1] They demonstrate a heart devoted to God and radical obedience.

Asbury Quotes

Lord make us humble, watchful, and useful to the end of our lives!

My earnest prayer is that nothing contrary to holiness may live in me.

When you go into the pulpit, go from your closets. Take with you your hearts full of fresh spring water from heaven, and preach Christ crucified and the resurrection, and that will conquer the world.

We must reach every section of America, especially the raw frontiers. We must not be afraid of men, devils, wild animals, or disease. Our motto must always be FORWARD!

At the present I am dissatisfied. I judge we are to be shut up in cities this winter. My brethren seem unwilling to leave the cities, but I think I will show them the way... I am determined to stand against all partiality. I have nothing to seek but the glory of God; and nothing to fear, but his displeasure... I am determined no man shall bias me with soft words and fair speeches: nor will I fear the face of man... even if I have to beg bread from door to door... I will be faithful to God, to the people, and to my own soul.

The reason why the Lord started speaking to our team in Kona about the circuit riders was so that we would notice how their lives illustrated the teachings and life of Jesus modeled in a generation that had a profound impact in history. The more we read, the more we saw the Sermon on the Mount alive in a breed of believers.

The more we studied, the more we were challenged in our own lack of "Jesus culture." It is all about Him, and this is what made the circuit riders such a meek but powerful force in human history. Could it be possible that we are being called to do this again today? Of course! It must be! When the truth of the Scriptures is whole-heartedly agreed upon and lived out, the impact on culture has always been profound. Our heart is to impact the culture for Jesus today in a profound way and to see a spiritual revolution.

To understand what this looks like we dug into the terms *culture* and *revolution*.

Culture

War rages around us. Ephesians 6:12 says,

> For our struggle is not against flesh and blood, but against the rulers, against the authorities, against the powers of this dark world and against the spiritual forces of evil in the heavenly realms.

The battle that we fight is not a *physical* battle, but rather an *ideological* battle for the hearts and minds of a generation. Thoughts give birth to ideas. Ideas give birth to values. Values give birth to actions. These actions are either determined by the redeemed mind in captivity to Christ (Romans 6:18), or by demonic arguments in the spiritual realm (2 Corinthians 10). The results of these influences manifest in the culture.

Culture can be defined as "the customary beliefs, social forms, and material traits of a racial, religious, or social group" or "the set of shared attitudes, values, goals, and practices that characterizes an institution or organization."[2] These values in a culture dictate our actions. We live in a fierce battle. Which culture will prevail? Will it be a culture of lies that leads to slavery to sin, or a culture of truth and therefore slavery to righteousness? The stakes are high. It is literally a life and death struggle. Slavery to sin will result in death. A culture of righteousness will lead to the glory of God, abundant life, and His kingdom on earth as it is in heaven (Matthew 6:10).

Revolution

Revolution can be defined as "a fundamental change in political organization; the overthrow or renunciation of one government or ruler and the substitution of another by the governed" or "a fundamental change in the way of thinking about or visualizing something; a change of paradigm."[3]

The revolution we seek is not a violent one, nor are we just seeking a political revolution. We are talking about a revolution of culture in which one value system, based on lies and deceptions, is replaced by another based on the truth of the Word of God. Let us not grow weary or lose an ounce of hope. Let us not create our report card on the influence of the kingdom of God from headlines or news channels. Rather, let us fall on our knees, embrace humility, wield the sword of repentance, and move back into alignment with the culture of the King!

Hope lies in the ever-present reality that the Lord is ready to move on behalf of a humble, renewed church. He is not reluctant to move in our cities and nations. Instead, He waits for us to overcome our reluctance and move into full agreement with His desires to revive and reform.

This cultural revolution begins in the hearts of individuals, spreads to the family, invades the bride of Christ, and soon becomes an irresistible force in our societies. It *must* first be real in our hearts to have any authority to invade our work places, universities, and homes. We are dreaming of a culture that creates a landing pad for the glory of God!

Culture is the Working Out of His Lordship

1 Thessalonians 4:1–2 says,

> Finally, brothers, we instructed you how to live in order to please God, as in fact you are living. Now we ask you and urge you in the Lord Jesus to do this more and more. For you know what instructions we gave you by the authority of the Lord Jesus.

Dream with me about what would be possible and what life would be like if we lived according to the culture of the kingdom—the culture set forth in the Bible and reiterated by the Spirit throughout history. Imagine a marriage, a family, a church, a community, or a city that agreed on something as simple as the cultural value taught in Ephesians 4:29:

> Do not let any unwholesome speech come out of your mouths, but only what is helpful for building

others up according to their needs, that it might
benefit those who listen.

To align with this value, news channels would have to change
drastically or shut down; many of us would have to relearn how
to talk and what to talk about. Imagine the life that would result
from only being able to speak that which is beneficial. Proverbs
15:4 says,

> The tongue that brings healing is a tree of life, but a
> deceitful tongue crushes the spirit.

How different would our lives and relationships be if every word
that came out of our mouths were from the tree of life? How
different would the church appear to the world? How different
would our families be?

If most of us were truly honest, we would acknowledge that a
fair amount of what we say in a single day actually "crushes" the
human spirit. We inadvertently partner with the demonic realm
when this ungodly culture is celebrated and empowered through
our lives. On the other hand, when we agree that wholesome
speech is the only speech that honors Jesus and benefits others,
then a culture of life will explode. This kind of culture becomes
infectious. Every human on the planet desires to live in this kind
of environment.

When the teachings of Jesus are lived out, He gains Lordship and governance over His people. This is where spiritual revolution begins to unfold. When we use our words to edify, trees
of life are planted and joy is released, breaking the strongholds of
hate and rejection. Many will experience new life and the love of

God. The tongue becomes bridled to the Lordship of Jesus. He becomes enthroned in conversations and relationships.

The same could be said for the kingdom value of faith. When faith is released in a community, it starts to dictate actions, thoughts, and words, thus creating culture. When a culture of faith has been created, then the supernatural begins to flow, dreams begin to be fulfilled, risks are taken, God gets glory, and the kingdom advances.

If faith is truly to become a cultural value within a community, then the spirit of unbelief must be viewed and dealt with as sin. This strength of commitment is what leads communities, families, and individuals of faith to be able to accomplish more for the kingdom than we as the Church have in the recent past. When faith becomes the cultural norm, and unbelief is repented of, Jesus is enthroned.

In this kingdom culture, no longer does human reason win over faith or the impossible rule out the possible. He gets to determine our actions and He defines what is possible. A faith-centered community like this will be on the verge of something massive.

Once again, dream with me of the possibilities for a whole generation madly in love with Jesus, eager to do anything He says, and devoted to a culture laid out in Bible truths. Imagine what power these individuals and communities would release through their fragrant culture. Could anything be so attractive to God and mankind? We believe this is a season where God is highlighting aspects of kingdom culture that the body as a whole is lacking. If these are fully restored, freedom and fruitfulness will abound.

I propose that we agree on several things:

- Truth is self-existent, knowable, and manifest in the God-man, Jesus (John 1).

- All of Jesus' teachings are true and livable. No command is too burdensome or impossible to live out (Deuteronomy 30:11-16).

- Anything opposite of revealed truth is sin and requires confession and repentance.

- Culture is created in either disagreement or agreement with these truths.

- If we choose to live according to the truths of the Bible, we will create a culture of heaven on earth (James 1:25; Matthew 7:24-27).

- This culture creates individuals and communities living in Jesus' loving Lordship.

- When Jesus is Lord, any other spiritual governance is overthrown in our lives and communities, and He alone becomes the One with our total allegiance.

- Lordship and allegiance lead to revival, revolution, and great fruitfulness for the cause of Christ!

Repentance Starts a Culture Shift

Before moving on to the revolutionary topics in this book, one thing must be highlighted and cannot be ignored. In order for a true culture shift to take place in our lives—first individually, and then reflected in our churches and communities—we must begin to pick up the sword of joyful repentance. I say *joyful* because repentance removes every obstacle that would hold us back from the fullness of what Jesus died to release in our lives. I say *repentance* because it is the right response to sin and compromise.

We cannot be afraid to call sin, sin. Only when it is really called what it is can it be properly dealt with. When we grasp that believing and living under lies and deception is actually sin, then we will cease to waiver in our commitment to true Bible-revealed kingdom culture.

We must live in an environment of grace where there is a freedom to fail. However, we must also understand that there is an appropriate response to failure. Only then can grace release its full power. We are free to fail, but we must respond appropriately when we do. Repentance is that response.

We don't need to move into condemnation, shame, or hours of endless counseling every time we fail. We just need to return to the truth of the gospel, repent, and come into alignment and allegiance to Jesus. Only when conviction increases to Biblical proportions can we actually live in kingdom culture.

It is not easy to live out these values. If it were, we would never have departed from them. But we are in a war, and repentance is one of our greatest weapons! When we realize that sin is only robbing us of the fullness of all that Jesus died for, then we begin to step into joyful repentance.

Jesus provides a river of pleasure while sin is a mud puddle of misery. Who in their right mind would not do whatever it takes to move beyond the mud puddle and immerse themselves in the river of delights? This is joyful repentance.

Revival is Now

Let's be really honest about the days we live in and the need for an urgent generation to arise and declare that revival is now. We are not hoping for something to change. It's far too late for wishful thinking. The battle over the hearts and minds of a generation is raging with greater force than a tornado. Billions are on the verge of a Christ-less eternity. Many are napping in an apparently pleasant summer calm not aware of a tsunami building just off the coast. Others see the reality of the tsunami but ignore it hoping it will go away like a bad dream, reluctant to believe anything might interrupt the bliss and sunshine. It is time to wake up. It is time to declare, "Revival is now."

This is an hour to "never be lacking in zeal, but to keep our spiritual fervor serving the Lord" (Romans 12:1). This is a day to be ever watchful and waiting, alert to all the Lord is doing. Desperate hours call for desperate measures. What I am *not* saying is that we should panic. This would be a fear-filled response to reality. What I *am* saying is that we must awaken and carry the same urgency that God has in His heart.

This generation must be ready to stand in the face of anything that may come: persecution, hardship, trial…anything. We must be victorious in difficulty, humble in victory, bulletproof to accusation and criticism, and yet tenderhearted to the accuser and the critic. We must never believe that just because we grew up in a bubble of relative peace and safety, affluence and blessing, that it will always be that way. We must never equate our material blessings with God's approval of our nation's ways. Much of our behavior is grievous to Jesus, but things are changing. The gospel never gives up, love never fails, and revival is now!

In this first volume of *Culture of Revival*, we will be high-lighting aspects of endurance, tenderheartedness, overcoming, and prevailing love. The title could easily read "A Life That Overcomes" or "A Faith That Endures." Our generation must recover the timeless truths that have taken the gospel all over the world on the backs of heroes of history. What made them men and women of steel? What caused their fruit to remain? These are the culture components we will be exploring.

As we begin this journey together in the pages of this first book, we will be looking at different aspects of the culture of the King and thus the culture of His kingdom.

Before you continue reading, I encourage you to take a moment and submit to the revolutionary power of the Holy Spirit in your own life. If you don't, these will simply be words on a page—catch phrases and repeated revelation. The world does not need more bandwagon slogans. We need a move of God! We need a culture shift! We need a revolution. Please join us in praying this simple prayer as you embark on this journey with us:

Jesus, You are the ultimate revolutionary! The culture You taught and lived was the ultimate expression of heaven on earth. I ask You, eradicate every value, lie, or half-truth that is out of alignment with You! Rip out every root of belief that has led to a culture of hell in my life, family, or city! I ask for a revolution—a violent overthrow—of any governance of my own mind and heart that I have given to the enemy of my soul.

I arm myself with the sword of joyful repentance and ready myself for anything the Holy Spirit would expose in my heart and mind that must be dealt with. Revive my heart and revolutionize my mind so that thousands would enter into Life because of me. I am Your joyful bondservant, commissioned to create a culture that gives You glory and creates a resting place for You to dwell, to rule, and to reign. Teach me Your ways! I desire to be Christ-centered above everything else in life! Open my mind. Open my heart. Open my eyes. Open my ears. Amen.

ABOUT THE AUTHOR: Andy Byrd and his wife, Holly, have dedicated their lives to spiritual awakening in a generation and in the nations. They work with a group of life-long covenant friends committed to consecrated community, Christ-centered living, revival, and cultural reformation. They are part of the leadership of University of the Nations, YWAM Kona, and have been with YWAM for thirteen years, traveling to many different nations with a heart to help raise up a revival generation to live in the confluence of prayer/intercession and gospel/mission. Andy and Holly have helped give birth to Fire and Fragrance ministries and the School of the Circuit Rider. One of the greatest delights of their lives and primary area of focus is their three children Asher, Hadassah, and Rhema, and the others that are still to come! Contact Andy at www.andybyrd.com, www.fireandfragrance.com, and www.thecircuitrider.com.

Culture of Revival

⌘

Volume 1:

Perseverance with Joy

❖

TWO

Married to the Land

By Jason Hershey

George Washington was a revolutionary. There was no two-year commitment or any other way out for him. It didn't matter...he didn't ask for one! He was fully engaged and undeterred by the growing pressures and risks of war. Victory was his only option. The completion of the mission was his only exit door.

Thomas Jefferson was a revolutionary. He stood up for what he believed and was willing to be branded a traitor by the British government. Jefferson penned the Declaration of Independence at age thirty. Did you catch that? He stepped into his destiny as a world changer at thirty. He understood that doing so made him a target for ridicule and possibly even death. Having counted the cost, he knew there was no turning back. Age meant nothing. He knew it was now his responsibility to carry this revolutionary call to the very end. He had to rise to the occasion.

My friends, it's time for a new generation of youth to rise and take personal responsibility for nations! Like Washington and Jefferson, we are in the midst of revolution, only this time our war is not physical—it is spiritual. Our lands are crying out for devoted intercession, our cities are begging for breakthrough, and we are in deep need for reconciliation with the Father's heart. These things will not be accomplished by quitters or by people who chase every hyped wind of new vision. This reconciliation can only come when a band of committed disciples come together under the banner of holy devotion and unwavering commitment in contending for His kingdom to come.

As a fellow revolutionary, I can only offer you my testimony, war story, and the amazing fruit that came through our community. Jesus has called me to the United States of America, to Washington, D.C., and specifically to the unborn. He has put a wedding band around my heart and covenanted me to His vision.

As an American, I received my call to the United States from Ezekiel 3:5-9.

> "You are not being sent to a people of obscure speech
> or strange language.... I will make your forehead like
> the hardest stone, harder than flint." —Ezekiel 3:5-9

Just prior to receiving this passage from the Lord, I had already committed my life to the mission field. I was so excited about all of the exotic places and far away nations I was about to explore, but this passage of Scripture implied that I wasn't going anywhere exotic! I wanted to gag.

A year later, I found myself crisscrossing the continental United States in a fifteen-passenger van with a full-time team of Youth With A Mission (YWAM) young adults. We called ourselves "The Revolution." We preached Jesus everywhere we went through drama, dance, music, and video. God began touching people's hearts, and all we knew to do was to offer an altar call as a response to God's kindness.

Our first outreach was to the northeastern United States. Ironically, or maybe divinely, we began the Sunday after September 11, 2001. The heart of Northeast America was obviously tender, which was reflected in the incredible response. In tears, many flocked to the front for prayer. No one cared about the format or style, people just responded with a new, fresh repentance, committing and recommitting their lives to Jesus and to the Great Commission. You can imagine just how stoked I was. I kept thinking to myself, "I'm a revivalist! Look at those responding!"

Oh how quickly the open door to a softhearted America was closed. I noticed a trailing off of responses to our message as early as the following January, just four months after the 9/11 tragedy. Nothing had changed in our Revolution team: it was the same people, the same heart, the same message—the right farmer with the right seed. It didn't take too long for us to realize it was the soil of people's hearts, not the effectiveness of our message, that had changed.

Ministry just wasn't as fun anymore. I began to think that maybe I wasn't the revivalist I thought I was. It's always exciting when the altars are full and sincere repentance is abundant, but now I had to reconcile with my feelings of seeming fruitlessness.

Even though the response to our message changed, I knew my call remained the same. It was time to pass the test of what kept me going in life: Was it the love of Jesus, or people's response to my message?

At this point, a good portion of me wanted to quit, but the Lord reminded me of the time He called me. He had told me that He would give me a "forehead of flint." I began to realize that my call came with an impartation; I no longer knew how to quit. My heart wouldn't let me. It soon went against my nature to think of grabbing a hold of the plow, only to look back. Jesus quickly became my only reward.

Tongue in cheek, it's always good to have a bargaining chip with God. The supreme bargaining chip—like a queen on a chessboard—is, "God, if You don't do (fill in the blank), I'm quitting!" With the "flint forehead impartation," I lost all my bargaining power; God knew I wouldn't quit. All of my selfish threats became nothing more than empty words. Unconditional obedience was now my only option. I began to understand that a full-on Jesus revolution in America was my only graduation to another call.

One of the final battle scenes from the movie *The Patriot* was a part of the multi-media message offered by The Revolution team. In this scene, the Revolutionary Army is suffering badly and the color guard begins to retreat. Mel Gibson's character wrestles the flag out of a soldier's hands and charges back up the hill screaming, "No retreat! No retreat!" A fellow officer follows his cry yelling, "Push forward men!" This scene marked me.

I was not the leader of The Revolution team; I was just one of the guys on the squad. By the end of that year, my team leader suddenly felt the Lord call him somewhere else. Was I done? Of course not! It was Jesus' vision, not my team leader's, to transform the United States. YWAM didn't call me to this; Jesus did. God rose up a new team around me and we pushed forward. No retreat! Isaiah 7:9 reminded me,

> "If you do not stand firm in your faith, you will not stand at all."

I believed that Christ Jesus, my Lord and Savior, had called me. I wanted to stand for what I believed in, but I didn't have a strategy. I didn't have influence. I didn't have half a clue as to how I was going to bring a Jesus revolution to America. Should we do street evangelism? A training program? Do we fast? Do we feast? Maybe a big event? I wanted to pull my hair out because every message I heard was telling me to do something different. I couldn't help but to think, "I only have twenty-four hours in a day, you know!"

Even though I had no idea what to do, I did know Jesus and received His Spirit. Deep inside, faith kept telling me, "The only way to be fruitful is to abide in the vine." Just keep going. I knew if I humbly held onto the hand of Jesus in simple obedience, He would lead me to change history. I just knew it. I hunkered into my personal prayer bunker and kept seeking the Lord. Galatians 5:25 has since become my life verse and consistently speaks comfort into my soul:

> Since we live by the Spirit, let us keep in step with the Spirit.

It's really not about strategy, structure, format, style, or expression. When we don't know what to do, it's comforting to know all we need to do is follow Jesus. Obeying the voice of God is simply the only way.

Washington, D.C.—Prayer with a Mission

Years came and went. We kept traveling, dancing, singing, preaching, praying, serving, and learning every step of the way! Four years later, Jesus led me to move to Washington, D.C., and dedicate my life to intercession. Our team moved and joined me in this new manifestation of ministry. Intercession is the place where the missions movement and prayer movement kiss each other. Intercession is prayer with a mission!

During His life on earth, Jesus intuitively knew that to make intercession, He had to go to Jerusalem. Through reading the Gospels over and over, I began to understand the intercessory authority that comes to those within a capital city. In fact, there came a time in Jesus' ministry when He set His face toward Jerusalem (Luke 9:51) and didn't turn back until He had finished His work of intercession for all mankind.

How can one not be impressed with the devotion, commitment, and loyalty of our wonderful Jesus? He left the glory of revival culture—heaven—and married Himself to the land of a fallen and broken earth. Jesus didn't leave the earth until He accomplished the freedom for the whole human race! He didn't just "go." He "stayed" until we were free!

Isaiah 62:1-7 throbs with the loyal heart of the Lord.

For Zion's sake I will not keep silent, for Jerusalem's sake I will not remain quiet, till her vindication shines out like the dawn, her salvation like a blazing torch.

The nations will see your vindication, and all kings your glory; you will be called by a new name that the mouth of the LORD will bestow.

You will be a crown of splendor in the LORD's hand, a royal diadem in the hand of your God.

No longer will they call you Deserted, or name your land Desolate. But you will be called Hephzibah, and your land Beulah; for the LORD will take delight in you, and your land will be married.

As a young man marries a young woman, so will your Builder marry you; as a bridegroom rejoices over his bride, so will your God rejoice over you.

I have posted watchmen on your walls, Jerusalem; they will never be silent day or night. You who call on the LORD, give yourselves no rest, and give him no rest till he establishes Jerusalem and makes her the praise of the earth.

This passage is where the phrase "married to the land" comes from. After several years of traveling ministry, Jesus called me to Washington D.C., to make intercession—to "marry the land" of America. Until then, I was merely "courting" America. A new level of devotion was needed for me to truly become an intercessor.

Jesus, the Author and Perfecter of our revival culture, modeled for us this great principle of marrying the land. He did not chase after the next hot vision but remained loyal to the land and the people to which He was called. If we want to be like Jesus, we must do the same.

I want to challenge you to look at your calling not just as what makes your heart leap, but also what makes your heart break. Hyped visions of how you are going to change the world tend to minimize the level of devotion that's required to actually do so. If Christ has broken you with His heart of love for a particular nation, city, university, or people, then that will come with an impartation of deep loyalty because Jesus' *agape* love is a love strengthened by loyalty! You will "marry" that land and you won't leave until it is established as a praise in the earth!

Jesus Christ our Lord's most fruitful weekend in ministry wasn't preaching, teaching, or healing, but simply a prophetic act of intercession. Upon moving to Washington, D.C., I realized that it was time for me to lay it all down, to simply "stand in the gap" (Ezekiel 22:30).

I remember imagining what people might have said to Jesus as He chose to lay down His life:

> *You have an incredible ministry, Jesus. You have an anointing like no one else. There are so many more that need to be delivered, healed, taught, and set free. What are you doing hanging on a cross?*

I once heard a quote from Evan Roberts' journal. God used Roberts to be a spark for a world-changing revival in Wales in 1904. He only preached a couple of years and then disappeared from public ministry. A quote from his journal was found after his death. It read, "I realized before man I could reach thousands, but before God I could reach the whole world." He committed his life to spreading the fire of Wales around the world through prayer and intercession.

Smashing the Idol of Acknowledgment

I went from standing on a stage several times a week to standing before the Lord in hiding. Was I really okay with being nameless and faceless? As it turns out, I was. I had received another beautiful impartation from God: the impartation of faith. Faith to know that the prayer of the righteous is powerful and effective. Faith to know that I was fruitful—even if it didn't manifest in that moment. He had given me faith that, if I made intercession from the capital city, I'd see a nationwide Jesus revolution sending missionaries around the globe.

This newfound faith got me in trouble though. Deep trouble. Criticisms started to pile up. Statements like, "You have a messianic complex!" and "You think that your prayers are going to just end abortion and turn this whole nation to Jesus?" and "You are spiritually prideful! Who do you think you are?" All the while, my forehead was like flint.

In Washington, D.C., my team joined me in dedicating our lives to day and night worship, fasting, prayer, and intercession. Naturally, with a lifestyle like that, the fire of God kept getting hotter and hotter within us. It was no coincidence that while we were in a "hot spot," the spirit of jealousy began to erupt and more criticism came. People were quick to point out everything they believed I was doing wrong. "Hershey's been given to extreme fasting!" All the while, my forehead was like flint. I reminded myself: *Jesus' words are more potent than the critics.* Intimacy with Jesus held me.

I found the criticism of being given to extreme fasting especially comical because it was so true. God had given me yet another impartation—the grace to fast. My soul began to rise up to meet the Lord in ways I had never experienced during extended fasts. The Spirit of revelation would cover me like a sweet fondue. The book of Daniel stirred me to believe that I was changing history as I fasted. Even though I've never had an angelic encounter, the faith within me would scream at me during my fasts, telling me that I was "moving angels into positions of breakthrough. Keep fasting!"

I began to feel like a well-trained warrior. Psalm 18:37 became one of my favorite pieces of Scripture:

> I pursued my enemies and overtook them; I did not turn back till they were destroyed.

With a forehead like flint, a shield of faith, the grace to fast, and my only reward being Jesus, I felt like saying to the Lord, "Put me in, Coach! I can play!" With my eyes fixed on Jesus and His words as my bread, I pushed forward.

Revolutions are violent, so you'd best be ready to fight. We are in a spiritual war, a war that can only be won by the gospel of peace. It is a war in which only the humble will survive. And you better not flinch when the enemy comes in like a flood. It's time for us to allow God to raise His standard against every evil through our lives:

> When the enemy shall come in like a flood, the Spirit of the Lord shall lift up a standard against him.
>
> —Isaiah 59:19 (KJV)

The Injustice of Abortion

If God calls you to a particular nation or people and you arrive only to find one specific injustice is killing over a quarter of them, do you think you might want to pray about that? Abortion became my Goliath.

Our intercession community grew over the next three years. A prophetic spirit rested upon us, and by 2008 we had grown to twenty-five people praying around the clock. That's when things got crazy. Real crazy.

Living in community is a landing pad for the Spirit of revelation. In the middle of the night, one of our young ladies, Colleen, was lying awake in bed. Her roommate, Danielle, rolled over in her sleep, looked at Colleen, said "Rizpah," and went back to sleep.

Imagine if that happened to you! Just live this moment for a second. You're wide awake in the middle of the night, silently laying on your bed, when your roommate rolls over, looks at you, whispers "Rizpah," and goes back to sleep. What in the world is Rizpah?

The next morning Danielle didn't remember a thing. It happened all in her sleep. Truth be known, Danielle did often talk in her sleep, but who or what was "Rizpah?" It seemed too random not to be God.

Within the next week, Lou Engle came through Washington, D.C., and met with our team. He challenged our team from 1 Samuel 21, which tells the story of a woman named Rizpah who stood 24/7 guarding the bodies of her dead sons. Lou challenged us, like Rizpah, to stand 24/7 at the Supreme Court throughout the summer, praying for the ending of abortion. It became clear to me that the word of the Lord to our community was "Rizpah." The words of 2 Chronicles 20:20 encouraged us:

> Have faith in the LORD your God and you will be upheld; have faith in his prophets and you will be successful.

Counting the cost, I had a decision to make. I made it, and we went for it. It was time to change history.

Smashing the Idol of Recreation

Partnering together with the Justice House of Prayer (JHOP), we stood vigil for the next one hundred days. It made sense that the short-term teams that JHOP was hosting should take the day watch, so our community took the nights and all of the weekends. Our weekends were doubly sacrificial, adding even more sacrifice to an already sacrificial lifestyle. The god of the weekend and recreation reared its ugly head.

> Gather to me this consecrated people, who made a covenant with me by sacrifice. —Psalm 50:5

The Fourth of July holiday landed smack in the middle of those one hundred days. You have to understand that there is no show like the Fourth of July fireworks show in Washington, D.C. Throngs of people from all around the world packed the

National Mall while we were in the middle of a season of focused fasting and prayer. This led to a very serious confrontation: Recreation vs. The Call to Pray. Fireworks vs. The Prayer Meeting. It was like two dueling cowboys in a western film: silent tumble weeds blowing by, saloon doors creaked on their hinges, and... BANG! Revolutionary, you'd better be ready when the idol of recreation comes knocking at your door. Recreation or revolution, which would you choose? I chose the prayer meeting.

I'd love to say, "That was the night the fire fell!" But honestly I can't remember that night having any special blessing or sense of breakthrough. That's the point though. It wasn't about getting something out of the meeting; it was about being faithful to the call of intercession on that season. It was a "fear of the Lord" issue. If God calls us to a consecrated season, then we must be faithful. Consecration simply means "set apart." Strict adherence to the Word of the Lord is the only proper offering we could give our wonderful Jesus. We were in the middle of a heaven-proclaimed season of consecration!

Do you know what it feels like to lead a missions community in a massively sacrificial mission and not see any tangible results day in and day out? Yesterday's testimonies aren't spurring you on because nothing seemingly happened yesterday. Intimacy with Jesus must be our only motivation.

Many people visited us and declared strong prophetic words over us during this season. In fact, three different people within a week's time declared that we were bearing "an embarrassing amount of fruit." To be honest, in the middle of the heat of the summer, it seemed like just words. Day in and day out, we stood. Not one headline changed and there was not one report of a clinic closing. Albert Einstein's definition of insanity kept running through my mind—doing the same thing over and over again and expecting different results—but I knew God had spoken, "Rizpah." Insanity? Maybe, but we kept going.

I cannot express the great respect I have in my heart for that incredible community of history makers. They poured it out, right along with me. At one point, Danielle stood in silent prayer for thirty-five hours straight without a break, one hour for every year since Roe vs. Wade, the Supreme Court case that legalized abortion on demand in 1973. After all that intercession, we were sure that we'd get a pro-life president and Congress that election year of 2008. We got the exact opposite!

So what happened? Does God not hear prayer? Does He not answer prayer? I knew that prayer was not an experiment. Sure, you may have a hypothesis, but in a true experiment, you don't know what the end results will be. Prayer is not an experiment because we know the end results. We knew God hears prayer, and yet for six months after Election Day in 2008, the answer to our intercession remained hidden.

An Eight-Million-Person Shift

It wasn't until May 15, 2009, a full year after starting the one hundred days of Rizpah, that Gallup came out with a startling poll. In the fourteen-year history of taking this poll, Americans were always more pro-choice than pro-life. However, according to their poll in 2008, America shifted seven percent, meaning that *over eight million* people had changed their minds on a very divisive issue! For the first time since they started taking that poll, America was now culturally more pro-life than pro-choice.[4]

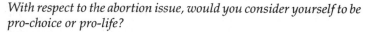

With respect to the abortion issue, would you consider yourself to be pro-choice or pro-life?

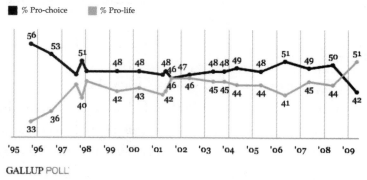

GALLUP POLL

Think of the stadiums you would have to fill to reach eight million people. Then, once you have them all packed in, every last one of them would need to repent and change their mind on a hugely politicized issue. Evan Roberts was right. "Before man I can reach thousands, before God, the whole world!"

Several other polling agencies decided to try and confirm these results, or possibly prove them wrong. Their polls came back with the exact same data. Pew Research, amazed at such a change, decided to study different demographics and events to try to figure how and why this happened. They came back with no explanation, but we knew the truth. God hears prayer!

The Rizpah team had changed history simply by standing in silent prayer in front of the Supreme Court. None of it was our idea. Glory to God alone! God spoke, we obeyed; history was made. To this day, America is getting increasingly pro-life all the time. Something broke in the heavens that summer. I wouldn't doubt that the night when the heavens broke was July 4. That was the night we kicked the god of recreation in the teeth. Oh that God would grant our generation the fear of the Lord. May our every prayer truly be a bomb bursting in air, giving proof through the night that our Jesus is still there! Don't you want to be a work of fire for Jesus?

Exhortation

That's just one of my war stories. Others have theirs. Even as I write this, I am still in Washington, D.C., contending for Jesus. It's been twelve years since I started this crazy journey, and it's not over yet. In fact, God spoke to me when I first moved to D.C. five years ago, saying that there would come a year that I would not leave the ten square mile boundary-line of the District of Columbia for the purpose of focused intercession for America. In the spring of 2011, Jesus made it clear that "2012 is the year!" So here I am, "married to the land," contending for America as well as for local breakthrough in the city. Even though I can't travel out of a ten square mile diamond, my "boundary-lines have fallen in pleasant places" (Psalm 16:6). This is what it means for me to abide in Jesus in 2012. In the vine, I am. The narrow way leads to the spacious place.

Recently I moved to what many would say is the "wrong side of the tracks" in Washington, D.C., what some have called a hard, dark place. High crime, poverty, and spiritual confusion are everywhere. It's a spiritual desert in desperate need of Jesus' transformational power. I believe that as I pray for a national Jesus revolution, I might as well live it locally. Isaiah 35 speaks of a desert turning into a fertile field. Let's get the flowers blooming!

We recently had a homeless man from Iran stumble into our prayer room. He wrote on a piece of paper, signaling that he was mute. We prayed for him and by the night's end, he was singing and praising God with us. Once we started communicating, he said he thought Jesus wasn't God, because He was God's Son. I explained to him the three-in-one God, and he totally understood it. The Spirit of revelation was on him. The desert is beginning to bloom.

All of us love to be in the river, the places of outpouring. It's glorious to be hanging out at the hot spots of our spiritual parents' breakthrough. I personally desire to camp out in the oasis of revival fellowship and never leave. The longing for heaven is written deeply within all our souls. We all have that longing, so it seems counter-intuitive to suddenly long for a desert. But that is exactly what happens.

Revolutionary, don't be taken off guard when the "cloud by day and fire by night" in your heart suddenly leads you away from the awesome revival community that you have grown up in and love. Your longing to be at the place of revival and awakening will give way to your longing to obediently follow Him into the next season of intimacy. His intimate presence is promised to you and will go with you wherever your assignment leads. Jesus is desperately looking to transform nations. He is longing for those who will say, "Here am I, send me!" Where are the ones that will cry out, "Oh God, give me a desert!"

Like Washington and Jefferson, a revolutionary knows when it's time to answer the call of Jesus and never look back. It's time for the Jesus revolution! Can you hear Him calling? You will be the one to turn a desert into a fertile field!

ABOUT THE AUTHOR: Jason Hershey lives in Washington D.C., with his wife Kimberlee and four children Cadence, Blaze,

Avella, and Anthem. They have been a part of Youth with a Mission since 1999 and have been pioneering a house of prayer in Washington D.C., since 2005. They are committed to living a lifestyle of prayer and mission, partnering with the Lord to see His promises released on the earth at any cost. As a family, they have a call to stand as intercessors for America, the unborn, and America's influence in the nations. Contact them at www.washingtonhop.org.

THREE

I Am a Voice

By Rick Pino

And from the throne proceeded lightnings, thunders, and voices. —Revelation 4:5 (NKJV)

How did John the Baptist—the one called to prepare the way for the Messiah—describe himself?

> **I am a voice** of one crying in the wilderness.
> —John 1:23 (NASB)

Throughout history, those whom God calls to turn a nation to Him have had a voice. My journey started in college after reading Ruth Ward Heflin's book *Revival Glory*. I had class from eight until noon, and when everyone else went to lunch, I went to my room. I purposed in my heart to fast lunch and seek the

Lord for two years. My roommate and I became so hungry for God that we started to pray together at 5 a.m., and then again from 10 p.m. to midnight.

We discovered incredible grace to seek God in this way. We prayed, "God, send revival to this nation," and "Lord, give me a breaker anointing." While I didn't see answers to these prayers manifest right away, it was a season of preparation.

Life moved very quickly from college prayer meetings to me being on a stage as a voice of worship and prophecy. To this day, when I feel like I'm losing my edge, or my heart is becoming jaded, calloused, or numb I go back to that season of preparation. I return to my first love and the plumb line of intensified seasons of prayer and fasting. From that place, the Lord sharpens my soul and opens my ears to hear His voice so I can represent His heart more effectively.

Luke 1:80 says that John was in the desert until his public appearance. God will take each of us into a uniquely-designed desert to prepare us for what's ahead. The Holy Spirit had poured His oil into John's heart for twenty years in the wilderness so that when the day of his public appearance came, John became a burning lamp for the nation to see. His whole life was lived in preparation for a single, short season—a moment in history that would close one Testament and open another.

He was the last of the old covenant prophets, and the first of the new covenant prophets. He was a wild man. His preaching was both piercing and encouraging:

> "Repent, for the kingdom of heaven is at hand."
> —Matthew 3:1-2 (NASB)

He gained so much influence in the nation that even Herod was shaking under the weight of his fiery teachings, radical life-style of fasting and prayer, and relentless pursuit of holiness. This man was a true sign and wonder to his generation. He was a voice crying out in the wilderness, preparing the people's hearts to receive Jesus.

The religious leaders of that day were so intimidated by him that they went out to question him. If only we could have heard the thoughts of these men as they made the journey out to the desert. They would have likely mused, "*If he really is of God, then why doesn't he dress the way we dress? Why doesn't he carry himself the way we do? If he really is of God, why is his ministry based in the muddy banks of the Jordan and not in the beautiful temple in the city? Why the long, messy hair, John? Why don't you drink wine? Why couldn't you attend your own parent's funeral? Where does your authority come from?*"

We learn a lot about John from the questions the priests asked and the answers he gave.

> Now this was John's testimony when the Jewish leaders in Jerusalem sent priests and Levites to ask him who he was. He did not fail to confess, but confessed freely, "I am not the Messiah."
>
> They asked him, "Then who are you? Are you Elijah?"
>
> He said, "I am not."
>
> "Are you the Prophet?"
>
> He answered, "No."

> Finally they said, "Who are you? Give us an answer
> to take back to those who sent us. What do you say
> about yourself?"—John 1:19-22

Humility, I's and Eyes

A true heart of humility marked John's life. He had a deep understanding of who he was, and he knew who he was not. When asked, "Are you the Christ?" instead of pretending to be someone he wasn't, he humbly confessed in front of all who listened that day, "I am not the Christ." Not only did he deny that he was the Savior, but he said things like, "I am unworthy to untie His sandals" and "You should baptize me, not me baptize You." Who else would be glad to hand over his entire ministry to another like John did when Jesus' ministry began to take off? John was not only a forerunner who prepared hearts to receive Jesus; his humility was an example to generations after him.

I remember the great evangelist Billy Graham once saying that you will never be more like Lucifer than when you become prideful because of the gifts, talents, and abilities that God has placed on your life. Lucifer was the anointed cherub who was called, equipped, and designed with splendor to be a living instrument of praise to the Lord (Ezekiel 28:13-14). He was adorned with so much beauty that his heart was lifted up inside of him (Ezekiel 28:17).

> "For you have said in your heart, 'I will ascend into
> heaven, I will exalt my throne above the stars of God;
> I will also sit on the mount of the congregation on
> the farthest sides of the north; I will ascend above the

heights of the clouds, I will be like the Most High.'"
—Isaiah 14:13-14 (NKJV)

There were five different "I's" that captivated Lucifer's heart:
- I will ascend into heaven
- I will exalt my throne
- I will sit on the mount of congregation
- I will ascend above the heights of the clouds
- I will be like the Most High

However, the "I" of John's heart sounded like this, "He must increase but I must decrease" (John 3:30). Unlike Lucifer, when John bowed the "I's" of his heart in humble submission to Christ, it opened the *eyes* of his heart in such a way that he was the first to see Jesus as "the Lamb of God who takes away the sin of the world" (John 1:29). Just like John, our "I's" will affect our eyes.

God gave John a gift to turn hearts just as He gave Lucifer a gift to create beautiful worship unto God. Through humility, John was able to discern how to use his gift wisely. While he could have easily turned hearts to himself like Lucifer, John used his gift to turn hearts to Christ.

The gift of God on a person's life will most certainly make room for them (Proverbs 18:16) and open doors of favor, blessing, and opportunity. The gift alone can often get the job done, but the dangerous thing is that it can get the job done outside of God's leading and grace. It is only when a person chooses humility that real virtue and substance can be imparted.

Gifted people who use their gifts for selfish gain are like a beautiful horse running to and fro doing whatever it pleases. The horse is of no use to the master because it has not been broken for battle. The master would rather use a steed that has a broken will than the strongest, most beautiful steed that does not. Not until the horse is broken and his will submitted to what the master desires, is he able to be of any good for battle.

Being broken isn't always a bad thing. In this case, broken is beautiful. It is time for this gifted generation to allow true humility to break their carnal will so that Jesus has a whole host of war horses ready for spiritual battle.

John was divinely gifted with the spirit and power of Elijah to turn hearts through his voice. However, John's identity was not caught up in the power or beauty of his gifting. John's identity was caught up in the resounding phrase, "He must increase and I must decrease."

Oh, if only a generation would realize, as John did, that every good and perfect gift comes from the Father of lights (James 1:17). How could we prostitute the pure gift of God for our own pleasure when it has only been entrusted to us for us to steward? It all comes from Him and it is all for Him.

Confidence in the Word of the Lord

The second question John was asked that day at the Jordan River concerned a well-known Old Testament prophecy: the return of Elijah before the day of the Lord (Malachi 4:5-6). John had confessed he was not the Christ, so the priests asked him if he was Elijah (John 1:21). Many were seeing that John was no ordinary preacher like those of the synagogues. His words carried authority. Like arrows soaring through the air, they would strike the heart with the flaming weight of conviction. One could only imagine the people whispering as they witnessed this burning vessel of fire, "Who is this man? Is this Elijah?" John displayed incredible humility in his answer, "I am not," knowing full well that the spirit and power of Elijah indeed was upon his life.

Thirty years before this scene, we see John's father, Zacharias, fulfilling his priestly duties in the temple. Suddenly the angel Gabriel appears to him and begins to prophecy about his unborn child:

> He will also go before Him in the spirit and power of Elijah, 'to turn the hearts of the fathers to the children,' and the disobedient to the wisdom of the just, to make ready a people prepared for the Lord."
>
> —Luke 1:17 (NKJV)

How many times might John have heard these words as a child, "You have the spirit and power of Elijah to turn this nation back to God." Parents often pray over their children, but if an angel appeared to me and prophesied about my daughter's birth, I would do nothing less than wash her in that angelic prophecy day and night until she was baptized with the reality of her destiny.

I'm convinced this word was spoken over John hundreds of times during his childhood. It is also my conviction that part of the reason John pressed through his years in the wilderness was because he could hear the words of his parents as a young boy, "You have the spirit and power of Elijah to turn this nation back to God." He must have thought, "I must never quit contending, and I must not relent in my pursuit of this word. Surely what was spoken over me by God will happen one day."

The archangel Gabriel prophesied "the spirit and power of Elijah" over John before his birth. His parents declared "the spirit and power of Elijah" over him as a child. However when he was asked, "Are you Elijah?" he answers, "I am not." Did he say this because he didn't believe the words of Gabriel concerning his destiny? I don't think so. John operated on a higher level of revelation and a deeper level of humility than to simply answer with a puffed up phrase like, "Haven't you heard of the angelic prophecy before my birth?" John knew that he was the Elijah whom God had promised and not the Elijah the crowds foolishly dreamed up.

Not too many people I know have had an angelic prophecy proclaiming their destiny before their birth. But God *has* spoken to each of us in His unique way. God has spoken to *you*, and to be the voice He has intended, you must carry the same confidence that John had so you can remain true to your identity in Christ—especially when the road gets very narrow.

During times of difficulty and uncertainty, God wants us to go back to the words He has spoken over our lives and receive our validation and confidence from Him. His promises will strengthen us and bring clarity about who we are, what we are to do, and also who we are *not*.

Identity in Christ, Not the Calling

There is a big difference between gifts and callings. A gift of God is the divine endowment to fulfill a cause or purpose; a calling of God is the invitation to use the gift for God's glory rather than man's. Truly, the gifts and callings are without repentance (Romans 11:29). Only when people submit their gifts to the purposes of God and answer their calling will they find themselves walking in the fullness of their destiny.

With humility and wisdom, John denied being the Christ; he denied being Elijah. So they asked him, "Are you the Prophet?" and again John said, "No" (John 1:21). However, it is my conviction that it would be impossible for one to be gifted with power to turn hearts and not be called a prophet. Why else would the Father give that gift in the first place? Surely not to turn hearts to carnal things or mere men. For the gift to turn hearts has been solely given by the Father for one purpose: to turn hearts to Jesus, the beloved Son of God.

Let's take a look at what Jesus had to say about John's prophetic calling.

> "But what did you go out to see? A prophet? Yes, I say to you, and more than a prophet. This is he of whom it is written: 'Behold, I send My messenger before Your face, who will prepare Your way before You.' For I say to you, among those born of women there is not a greater prophet than John the Baptist."
> —Luke 7:26-28 (NKJV)

The words of Jesus confirm that not only was John a prophet, but he was the greatest prophet born of women. It was not merely an angel that said this, but Jesus Christ Himself, the Son of the living God. What made him the "greatest" prophet? Up until that time every prophet had declared, "The Messiah is coming! The Messiah is coming!" John was the first to say, "He is here!"

The reason that John answered "no" to the question about being a prophet was because he had the prophetic eyes to see that the true Prophet, Priest, and King was already here. The very spirit by which John would prophecy belonged to Jesus—for the testimony of Jesus is the spirit of prophecy (Revelation 19:10).

Here was the reason that John had been born. He was the prophetic announcer that the One they had been waiting for had finally arrived. How could his identity be wrapped up in his calling as a prophet after he had seen the true Prophet? How could we have our identity wrapped up in our prophetic calling when we have seen the One who has invited us to fulfill it? Foolish is the person who places their identity in the calling and not the Christ.

Shatter the Silence

What I would give to be there in the moments after John's answers!

> "I am not the Christ." They asked him, "What then? Are you Elijah?" And he said, "I am not." "Are you the Prophet?" And he answered, "No." Then they said to him, "Who are you, so that we may give an answer to those who sent us? What do you say about yourself?"
> —John 1:20-22 (NASB)

Then all of a sudden John gives them an answer. It is not the one they are looking for, but it is the correct answer.

> He said: "**I am a voice** of one crying in the wilderness, 'Make straight the way of the Lord,' as Isaiah the prophet said." —John 1:23 (NASB)

There it is. *I am a voice.*

This answer, though short, summed up the oceans of John's heart into a single drop of truth. *I am a voice. I am not a name. I am not a face. I am not trying to be what you think I should be. I am pressing to be what He has destined me to be. I am not trying to be popular; I am trying to be obedient. I am not trying to build my kingdom; I am announcing that He is here to build His.*

Truly John was a voice crying out in the wilderness. He was a spiritual alarm clock that released a sound that shattered four hundred years of silence. The living breath of God was being blown through a vessel that had died and had hollowed out his insides from any pride as to make room for God. We need the voices crying in the wilderness of culture, in the wilderness of perversion, in the wilderness of our broken governmental systems to arise with a sound that shatters the silence. We need voices of Godly influence to begin to sound the alarm!

Popularity vs. Influence

A true voice of Godly influence does not come by self-promotion. If John had been relying on self-promotion, he would not have carried the same weight of influence. He denied all the questions, humbled himself, and pointed people to Jesus. However, we live in a day where many are trying to point people to themselves by building their kingdoms and "castles in the sands" of popularity and self-promotion. We must realize that popularity and influence are two different things.

Popularity is simply to have the approval of people, but influence is to have power to affect people. Popularity changes with the wind, but influence can change the direction of the wind.

Just because someone is popular doesn't necessarily mean they are influential.

Ancient heroes of the Bible were seldom popular.

- Joseph was sold into slavery by his brothers because of jealousy.
- Daniel was cast into the lion's den for having a prayer life.
- David was rejected by his family and not even invited when the most famous prophet of the day came to his house.
- Elijah was hated by Ahab and Jezebel and was threatened to be killed because he chose to stand for righteousness.

All of this occurred because these men were unpopular. However, these heroes had a common denominator that was the game changer for all of their situations: influence in the heavenly realm.

- Joseph's Godly influence opened the door of favor, which promoted him to a place of authority so the same brothers that sold him into slavery would be saved in the time of drought.
- Daniel's Godly influence in the place of prayer and fasting saved him from the lion's mouths. When Daniel fasted, even the lions had to fast.
- David's Godly influence caused him to be empowered with a supernatural anointing for

victory in war. The boy rejected by some now was accepted as the giant fell that day.

- Elijah's Godly influence turned a nation back to God. He was entrusted with the ability to set his face to stand for righteousness, no matter the cost.

You must be okay with never having your voice, talents, or abilities acknowledged by others around you. If you do what you do to be seen by anyone other than God, then you are missing the will of God for your life. Instead, focus on becoming famous before the throne of God. If you can influence heaven, you will have no problem influencing men and women on earth.

If God has given you a voice, you must be careful not to sell out your voice to compromise for money or fame. When I first started leading worship, different production companies approached me about signing with them. I'm not against these companies in any way, but it wasn't for me. If I had gone that route, I would have been betraying my own heart.

For me, part of the process was dealing with the question, "Should I do it like everyone else, or the way I know is right for me, and then trust God to supply everything else?" The narrow road is indeed narrow. Not many people find it and few choose to walk it. When I've trusted God and gone with what was true for me, I've found the biggest blessings. I would not do what I've done differently.

Overcoming the Opposition

Religious spirits that want to keep the Church boxed in will always oppose forerunners like John the Baptist. Religious spirits keep us in the old; forerunners are called to break us into the new. Don't be alarmed when religious spirits come against you. Stay the course and use your voice.

A number of years ago as I was preparing to lead worship in another city, I sensed that I was going to encounter opposition. So I returned to my plumb line of prayer and fasting for three days. The Lord told me specifically, "No toleration of Jezebel," from Revelation 2.

When I arrived to lead worship, I told the pastor that God had given me a specific word and I asked if he wanted for me to share it with him. He said, "No, you just go for it." The meeting started and during worship I shared this word about no toleration of Jezebel.

After worship the guest speaker got up to speak. The first thing he said was, "Where's Rick?" I was in the back of the room and raised my hand. He continued, "Great to see you, Rick. And I just want to let you all know that everything Rick said is heresy. And Rick, I'm going to talk to you later about this."

After the meeting, I got into the car with a friend of mine who told me, "There is a very popular magazine here in town that promotes abortion, women's rights, promiscuity, and other similar themes. The magazine is called *Jezebel* and it's sweeping the city."

Releasing the word of the Lord and being publicly humiliated in front of everyone was an encouragement that I was doing something right. If you've heard from God and He tells you to say something, speak it out. Strengthen yourself with the words of Jeremiah 1:7-8 (NKJV):

> "For you shall go to all to whom I send you, and whatever I command you, you shall speak. Do not be

afraid of their faces, for I am with you to deliver you,"
says the LORD.

Consecration Fuels a Voice of Influence

As the Lord is with you to develop your voice, it is important to remember that there are not simply good influences and bad influences. There are different levels of influence. In his brilliant book, *Fasting for Spiritual Breakthrough*, Elmer Towns says that your level of consecration will determine the level of your voice of influence.

For instance, say Peter has a "level two" consecration. He loves God, but watches movies that he shouldn't watch. He lives very loosely with his walk with Christ, and he isn't very careful about how he speaks to others. Peter will also have a "level two" voice of influence. He may possibly lead one friend to Christ a year, in a good year, but never do anything much more than that.

Now take Robert. He has a "level seven" consecration. He has decided to seek God during times he would have usually watched a movie in addition to his daily devotional time. He is consistent to pray for all of his friends and family. Robert does his best to fast three times a month to seek God for a deeper revelation of the Word of God. Robert will also have a "level seven" voice of influence. He is being powerfully used by God in his city to stir people for prayer and worship, and is a respected leader because his character is upright and trustworthy.

John the Baptist had a "level ten" consecration and therefore was entrusted with a "level ten" voice of influence to shake not only his generation, but also the generations to come. His voice can still be heard crying out two thousand years later.

My friend Will Ford III says it like this, "To the measure that you sell out for your kingdom, that is the level of influence you will have in that kingdom." It goes both ways. There are people in the secular arena that have completely sold out to the kingdom of darkness and are being used at high levels of demonic influence to shake a nation.

It's time for a sold-out generation of level-ten believers to go to the wilderness of fasting, prayer, consecration, and extreme obedience, and come out with level-ten prophetic voices of fire that will shake the thrones of powers and principalities.

There is a difference between the level of influence and anointing that comes at the time of salvation and the level of anointing and influence that comes to those who take the kingdom by force. I encourage you to be one who seeks God and refuses to back down in your consecration until you see God's power break out in fullness. Like Isaiah, we need the coal of consecration to touch our unclean lips so that we can literally become the sent mouthpieces of God (Isaiah 6:5-6).

Lightnings, Thunders, and Voices

Rock stars don't proceed from the throne. Big churches don't proceed from the throne. Money doesn't proceed from the throne. What proceeds from the throne of God?

> And from the throne proceeded lightnings, thunders, and voices. —Revelation 4:5 (NKJV)

If we can get a voice proceeding before the throne of God, we will also be moving with the lightnings—the power of God— and the thunders—the authority of God. What does it mean to be a voice proceeding before the throne of God? It is the difference between being gifted, called, and anointed, and being a sent one who is mantled with authority like Elijah to call for the heavens to open over a nation and pour forth the rains of revival.

Be a Voice

I leave you with the lyrics of a song that God gave us concerning being a voice. Pray these lyrics over your heart as you read them and make this the prayer of your life: that you will be a level ten voice of godly influence; that you will arise from the wilderness of your generation mantled with authority; and that you will shake the thrones of the powers and principalities for the glory of Christ!

[Verse 1]
The Pharisees could not see this man was sent from God.
They asked him, "Are you someone great?" but he said "I am not.
You brood of vipers, don't you see that I am not the Christ?
I am one who's gone before to lay down my life."

[Chorus]
"I am a voice, I am a voice,
Crying out in the wilderness."

[Verse 2]
Your pride and gift alone will not make you His choice.
He's looking for the ones who only want to be a voice.
So keep on climbing, climbing all your ladders to the top.
But don't you know that in the kingdom, down is the way up?

[Verse 3]
He's looking for the ones who do not care about the cost,
Denying earthly pleasures, finding pleasures of His heart.
So lay down Your life, become the highway of the King.
The narrow path will be your crown, authority your ring.

ABOUT THE AUTHOR: Rick Pino is the founder of Fire Rain Ministries, a "voice crying out" ministry who, for the past seven years, has been calling people to lives of radical love, radical holiness, and radical devotion to Jesus. His music is known for being militant, joyful, intimate, and prophetic. Rick is also the co-founder of "Fire on the Altar" regional worship events, which are fifty-hour gatherings of non-stop worship in the heart of the tabernacle of David. During these gatherings there is only one agenda: to bring the Lord an offering of unbroken love. Currently, Rick and his wife, Lindsey, live in Dallas, Texas, with their daughter Zoey. Contact Rick at www.rickpino.com.

✳

FOUR

To Those Who Overcome

By Amy Sollars

It was a frigid fall day in the wilderness of Alaska, and I was journeying down a forested path that eventually emerged onto a beach. As I stood beside the waters, surrounded by magnificent mountain peaks and white-capped ocean waves, I heard a sound. This was no ordinary sound. I realized what I was hearing was not coming into my natural ears, but rather it was coming into my spiritual ears. It was unlike anything I had ever heard.

The depth of it gripped me. The sound was coming from every direction. Suddenly, the presence of the fear of the Lord gripped my soul. It felt like the earth was groaning—the trees, water, mountains, and even the ground where I stood. I remembered Romans 8:22: "For we know that the whole creation has been groaning…"

In the midst of this groaning creation, something was spoken with such intensity that I will never forget it. The groaning creation was calling to me, "Do you know who you are?"

I was rattled to my bones—this was about identity and destiny. Romans 8:19 says,

> For the creation waits in eager expectation for the children of God to be revealed.

In this encounter, I was gripped with the understanding that my life had greater meaning than I had known. From there, I embarked on a journey of discovering who I am in Christ. For too long the lies, labels, and stereotypes of man and the enemy had tagged me, but in this journey I've found "me" in Jesus' liberating power.

The Early Days

In 1980, I was born in Sitka, Alaska, the fifth generation of Alaskans in my family. One week after my birth, I was flown to the remote fishing grounds where my father worked six months out of the year so that he could meet me. Two years later, my parents married shortly after the birth of my sister. They developed this grand idea of moving our small family out into the Alaskan wilderness. The purpose was to live off the land and be self-sustaining.

With my father gone half the year on a fishing boat, my mother was left alone with two little girls, no running water, and very little electricity from a generator. When I was six, my brother was born, and we moved from one remote place to another to do it all over again. This was the only life I knew. It wasn't until later that I came to understand how rare and different my life really was.

My father was not a Christian; my mother was from a Baptist background, learning her way back to the Lord. She taught us the basics of salvation and provided simple teachings through Bible stories. I don't remember the day I prayed the salvation prayer, but I do remember knowing God. My mother says I sang before I talked and when I learned to talk, I never stopped. I had a close awareness of God, and I remember simply "knowing things" I thought everyone else already knew. Later, I discovered this was actually the Lord speaking to me.

The Battle for My Soul

In many ways, I was a normal little girl and in many ways I was not. Around age six, I started to gain weight. We lived in remote Alaska, so my mom thought I would grow out of it. I never did. By the time I was twelve years old, I was close to two hundred pounds and no one really knew why. My dad's prolonged absences were causing problems in my parents' marriage.

When I was in third grade, my mom moved us kids to town for the winters. Public school was a harsh environment. I had experienced unconditional love from my family and didn't understand that being overweight was socially unacceptable. The insults began and the wound grew deeper with each passing comment.

I lived the next five years in horrific torment as the door to Satan's lies was opened and flooded my soul. It first began as simple thoughts. In a short while, it escalated to demonic torment where I was hearing voices in my head all the time, telling me horrible lies and trying to convince me to kill myself. It then went from just hearing voices to seeing demons come into my room and speak to me.

A couple of years into the demonic torment, I couldn't handle the oppression any longer, so I loaded a gun and put it to my head. I went to pull the trigger and the audible voice of God broke through the room and said, "NO!" I suddenly fell asleep and woke up the next day. Again and again I tried to kill myself, and every time the Lord broke in at the last moment to prevent me from going through with it.

I did not really want to die; I just wanted to end the torment I lived in. I thought if I ever told anyone, they would send me away to a mental ward and label me insane. I assumed I was crazy. No one knew. When I finally did tell a friend, she freaked out and couldn't handle the reality of the horror I lived in.

Jesus the Great Deliverer

When I was fourteen, we returned to the wilderness and my life continued to unravel. I would cry myself to sleep every night, stuffing a pillowcase into my mouth so my family would not hear me screaming from the deep pain that I felt.

Following my sixteenth birthday, I was at a small church in Alaska that I attended occasionally. That weekend there was a guest preacher who was ministering on freedom. I sat there listening, and my soul was gripped in the most intense wrestle. I could hear two competing voices: the enemy screaming lies and the Lord's tender whisper. I heard Jesus whisper to go forward for prayer while the enemy told me to stay put.

By God's grace, I somehow found myself up front. As the minister began to pray for me, immediately I started manifesting the demonic and a strange voice came out of me. The minister identified the evil spirit as the spirit of death. After about twenty minutes of praying, the spiritual war over my soul subsided. Suddenly, all of the evil spirits attached to me had quickly disappeared.

With tears streaming down my face, I turned to the church congregation, who sat in amazement, and said, "They're gone! Why is it so quiet in here?" I could not remember a time in my life when I was not tormented by the lies and noise of the devil. The quiet was so peaceful.

Everyday Journey of Freedom

After this dramatic freedom experience, I was set on a path towards the freedom to overcome. You might ask, "How could this happen to you?" You see, once you're saved by the blood of Jesus, Satan cannot possess your spirit—you belong to God. However, when you are in agreement with the enemy through lies or sin, he will affect your soul and body.

Satan's primary fear is that Christians will discover who they are in Christ and move in the fullness of their inheritance. The enemy tried to kill me before I ever had a chance to know this. Despite his greatest efforts, he lost, and the Lord taught me to overcome.

The truth is, things didn't change overnight. Despite my deliverance encounter, it wasn't like I could suddenly love myself completely. For so long I had lived with intense self-hatred. That way of thinking had become a pattern in my mind. I lived a life of rejection stemming from self-hatred.

It has been a long and winding journey of overcoming the pain and issues that accompany rejection. That day I started down the road to discovering who I am, and I decided right then and there that I was going to live for Jesus with my entire being. I knew I was meant to help set people free, even though I had no idea how to do it.

A New Gift and Its Mistaken Identity

In the following weeks, I came to realize that although the demonic voices stopped and the evil spirits were no longer tormenting me, I could still hear and see things. I would suddenly sense or "know" things about other people. I could "see" things in the spirit realm associated with the people around me. I began to freak out as it became very obvious that I was not going to live what most people knew as a normal life. Some leaders in my life helped me understand that I was not crazy, but rather that I had a gift from God. I had a prophetic gift, specifically in the area of being a "seer" (1 Samuel 9:9). Over the next few years, I began to learn how to use this gift.

My mistake was that I began to establish my identity, friendships, and my entire life on this gift. My deep-rooted fear, self-hatred, and insecurity caused me to cling to the gift more than Jesus. I had no idea who I was outside of being prophetic. All of my friends were developing relationships, getting married, and having kids. Those were also things that I wanted. I sat alone and overweight; no men were interested in marrying me.

The harder things got, the more I clung to the prophetic. As a result, much of what I prophesied lacked love because of my bitterness from years of rejection. I could easily see people's issues, and my words were often harsh. The words I shared were not a reflection of the Lord's voice and heart. I thought I was accurate in what I prophesied, but many times I was wrong in the way I reflected Him. I became judgmental towards the things I saw and experienced. Pastors became leery of me and rightly so. I perceived I was being rejected and felt alone, clinging to the only thing I had—my gift. Who was I?

Jesus, My Identity

After two years of public ministry, I was asked to step down and enter a season of discovery with God. Though my flesh fought it, I knew it was going to be a time of being disciplined and established by God as His daughter. In that season I fasted, prayed, and cried out to God to have His way in my heart and life. As a result, I fell in love with Jesus and my brokenness began to be transformed. I realized I had been prophesying out of my gifting. I had no idea of the Lord's heart for the people I was ministering to. At times, my ministry had served me rather than God or His people. I lost my desire to be known for my prophetic gift and I told Him that I did not care if I ever became a prophet. The only desire I had was to simply be a friend of God and lover of people.

I desired to be known for love, not prophecy. I did not want people to have an encounter with me; I wanted them to encounter Jesus. I started a journey of learning to love, and it changed everything. The way I spoke, prophesied, and ministered all changed. It changed the way I saw, felt, and loved. The Lord's heart for people and places gripped me in unimaginable ways. It was not about having details and grandiose words, but rather asking the Lord what was on His heart for this person, no matter how big or small the word seemed to me.

When this brokenness took place, I entered into one of the most amazing seasons of encounter that I have ever known. No longer was I seeing what the enemy was doing; I was seeing what heaven was doing. I was having the most life-changing and incredible experiences with God. I would invite the presence of the Holy Spirit, and He would come. I would encounter the Lord's heart and the Holy Spirit would give me visions and take me on adventures. I was changed forever as I saw the fire in His eyes—the eyes of fire that burned with love for me and for people. Revelation 1:14 says, "His eyes were like blazing fire." As I gazed into those eyes, I was ruined forever. It launched me into a life of overcoming through Christ.

The Battle for Faith and Kingdom Reality

Not long after this season, many medical issues began to escalate in my life. I continued to gain weight every year. One day, a doctor told me that my body was falling apart and he didn't think I would live beyond the age of forty.

I remember driving away from that appointment screaming out to God in frustration. Suddenly an overcoming faith welled up inside and I cried out, "If I die I die, but I will live all the days of my life for You, Jesus." I felt so alone in the battle and was at a loss for what was next. Everyone assumed the reason I was so overweight was because I had a food addiction and was living a very unhealthy lifestyle. But that wasn't the main issue of my health battle.

On Earth As It Is in Heaven

Every day I had to make a decision to choose truth over lies. My flesh screamed, "Give up!" One day I cried out to God for freedom and He said, "Amy, there is a reality of heaven and a reality of earth. When you are in agreement with the reality of earth, it keeps heaven from breaking in. But when you believe the reality of heaven, I will break in. Your circumstance may not change, but you will." From then on, I chose to walk in faith and no longer let my circumstances dictate who I was or what would happen to me.

As time progressed, I relied more on His faithfulness, and His authority in me grew stronger. I would look into the face of death and declare I would live. I refused to let the pain close my heart, but I choose to let it soften me and increase love more. Day in and day out I would ask the Lord what was on His heart. He would share His secrets with me. I still wrestled, but I refused to give up, knowing it was worth it no matter what.

Friendship, Accountability, Victory

A few years later the Lord led me to join Youth With A Mission (YWAM) to partner with friends Andy and Holly Byrd. In the first couple years, my medical issues escalated and the doctors told me I had approximately ten years to live. In love, Andy and Holly approached me and told me no matter what the doctors said or how impossible it was to lose the weight, they were not going to stand by and passively accept it. So the journey of their friendship and accountability began.

No matter how frustrated I got, they would not allow me to quit. They told me that breakthrough was possible. As a result of their help and God's grace, I entered into the greatest level of overcoming that I had ever known. At the beginning of this time, I weighed 390 pounds. I currently have lost 190 pounds! Death has lost its hold on me and I have overcome!

To Those Who Overcome

There are many rewards to overcoming. But the ultimate reward of overcoming is encountering Christ Himself (see Revelation 2-3). Knowing the love of Jesus in our lives is the key to living as overcomers. When we know that our identity is found in the revelation of Jesus, His kingdom comes to earth and anything in Him becomes possible.

The same spirit that raised Christ from the dead lives inside of us (Romans 8:11). When we enter into a saving relationship with Christ, we are given the power to overcome the world (1 John 5:4). If the same spirit of Christ that is in you has overcome the world, then what lie of hell or circumstance of the world can hold that power back? He lives inside of you and you are the generation on the earth that is meant to overcome and take your stand. Do you know who you are? Ask for the Lord's revelation for your life's destiny and stand firm in faith. If God is for you, then who can be against you? (Romans 8:31). This truth helps us to overcome.

I believe there is a new breed of overcoming Jesus lovers on the earth! They are the manifest sons and daughters of God. All creation is groaning for them, crying out, "Do you know who you are?" (Romans 8:19, 22). No circumstance of earth or lie of hell can keep you from walking in the fullness of God when you count the cost, say yes to Jesus, and learn to love.

I believe this new breed is a prophetic generation full of the spirit of Jesus with resurrection life running though their veins. The testimony of Jesus is the true spirit of prophecy (Revelation 19:10). We are called to live in a culture where prophecy always comes from a revelation of the love of Christ. Gone are the days where we exalt one man or woman, but here is the day where a whole generation is prophesying, declaring, hearing, seeing, discerning, and encountering Jesus! As we abide in His love, the prophetic flows in our lives. When we minister to people, they will not just encounter the prophetic, but will be changed by Jesus.

We need to have a culture where it is not about getting the next great prophetic word, but instead it's about overcoming in our life's circumstance to know Jesus and prophesy what He is saying. The true spirit of prophecy brings encounter with the man Christ Jesus. The more we fall in love with Him, the more prophetic we become.

Through the spirit of Jesus, we can understand the earth's times and seasons with the perspective of heaven. Through His love we are meant to become the most accurately prophetic people on earth. We become living prophetic words as we prophesy with our lives, living out the things we prophesy. We are not known for our call, the labels of man, or the accusations of the enemy—we are known by Jesus.

All across the earth the Lord is releasing dreams, visions, and encounters. His voice is going forth to the nameless and faceless, and they are releasing words that are changing the course of history. It's not about one person being prophetic; it's about a generation where the Spirit of the Lord has been poured out.

Joel 2:28 states that God "will pour [His] Spirit on all people. Your sons and daughters will prophesy." We are to live in a culture where we overcome and are postured for encounter.

Keys to Victory and the Overcoming Lifestyle

- **Repent**. Through the gift of repentance, remove any barrier of sin. This can also be in the areas of fear of what the Holy Spirit might say or do. If you have spoken against other people's encounters or against the way the Spirit has moved in someone else, it is time to repent and let go of any fear or judgment.

- **Surrender**. Give the Holy Spirit permission to do and say what He wants. Repent of the times you have said, "I will never..." and yield to the work of God in your life—however it may look.

- **Word**. Spend time in the Word of God and encounter Him through His Word. The Holy Spirit is the Author of the Bible. The more you keep God's Word in you, the stronger your foundation will be. Ask to experience the Holy Spirit while you are reading and studying. Hebrews 4:12 says, "For the word of God is alive and active. Sharper than any double-edged sword, it penetrates even to dividing soul and spirit, joints and marrow; it judges the thoughts and attitudes of the heart."

- **Worship**. Go deep into the place of worship: worship both corporately and individually. Some of my most amazing encounters happened in the context of worship. As we declare who the Lord is and love on Him, it opens us up for the river to flow.

- **Prayer.** Through prayer we can carry the burdens on God's heart. As we pray, God reveals more of His heart. He delights to reveal and guide us into His will.

- **Presence and waiting.** Practicing His presence can look different for different people. Sometimes I simply sit quietly in a room by myself. Sometimes I play soft music while I wait for His presence. I find a place without distraction and invite the Holy Spirit to come in. I love on Him and allow Him to love on me. I ask Him if there is anything He wants to show me. I submit my imagination and mind to Him. I am not waiting on Him for the purpose of gaining revelation, but when I surrender to His presence the revelation flows.

Spiritual and Practical Keys for Encounter

- **Peace and rest.** Peace is the gateway to visitation. You can't force a visitation from your flesh. Pure encounters happen when you are in peace. If you are striving, it cuts off the pure flow of God and you open yourself to hear and experience things in your soul and flesh and not with your spirit.

- **Asking and being "hungry."** Even in the place of peace, ask the Lord to give you encounters. It's okay to hunger and earnestly desire encounter, but you need to do this from a place of being secure in His love. Your encounters have nothing to do with your worth and are not the measuring rod of His love. Engage your faith and trust Him.

- **Purity.** Keep your gates clean. What you listen to and meditate on can affect the flow of encounter. When you don't guard your spirit, your encounters can be hindered. The things you do during the day can also affect your dream life. The more I am in His presence, the more active my spirit is in encountering Him.

- **Pray in the Spirit.** When you pray in the Holy Spirit (using the gift of tongues), it builds up your spirit man. It can activate encounter.

- **Accountability.** Be accountable to mature Godly men and women. You may not always find all that you experience in Scripture, but encounters cannot violate the overall guidelines of Scripture. Make sure you have trusted people in your life who will tell you whether or not you are hearing, seeing, and sensing things from the Lord.

- **Write it down.** Keep a journal or record so that you can remember the encounters. I have encounters all the time that I don't understand until some years later. When you are faithful with what He gives you, He will give you more.

My heart's cry is for you to understand that when you choose Jesus and truth, you will discover freedom in your identity and you will overcome the lies of the enemy. From the place of the Father's love, God has called you to overcome and live in a life-style of encountering Him every day.

ABOUT THE AUTHOR: Amy Sollars is a lover of Jesus who has given her life to see the kingdom of heaven released on the earth. She is one of the founders of the Fire and Fragrance and Circuit Rider schools. She carries a prophetic anointing and releases the heart of the Father over people and places. She has a heart to see people have a radical, intimate relationship with Jesus. Most of all, she longs to be a friend of God and for everyone to experience Him as a Friend. Another part of her ministry is in the area of prophetic worship as she sings spontaneous songs of the Lord. Amy travels and ministers all over the world with YWAM and other ministries. Contact her at www.amysollars.com.

❖

FIVE

Love Looks Like Something

By Jake Hamilton

It was by far the largest gathering of people I had ever played in front of, and I found myself more excited than nervous. I knew that I was created for this moment. I felt like I was waiting for Christmas morning. You know the drill. You know what's coming, you've been here before, but no matter how many times you've woken up to newly wrapped presents under the tree, it's always hard to sleep the night before.

We stepped up to sound check in the afternoon at the All State Arena in Chicago about the same time my wife's plane was landing at O'Hare. We checked each instrument, ran through a few songs in the set, and made sure that we knew, at least in

theory, which direction we would head. My wife arrived just before we were about to go on, and the arena steadily filled with the
young and the old seeking an encounter with the living God. I
gave my wife a swift kiss, she told me how excited she was, and I
headed on to the dimly lit platform to launch in to Bob Dylan's
"These Times They Are a Changin'."

I don't remember much about the set. It was sort of a blur
even after I tried to relive it through YouTube cuts of our forty-
five minutes on stage. It wasn't that I didn't enjoy it, or that I
didn't feel like it was anointed. And it's not that I'm trying to be
"Captain Humility." It's just that what took place the *following*
morning changed my life forever.

It All Begins With Love

I guess at this point a brief history would serve you well.
My wife and I met while planting a church in our hometown of
Rancho Cucamonga, California. It sounds cliché, but she was
my administrative assistant at the time we started dating. We
quickly realized we were meant for each other and less than a
year after our first date, we got married. We truly married into
ministry and maintained that way of life for nine years while we
planted a church, led a youth ministry, had three beautiful children, and started a house of prayer. All of this was before I recorded an album with Jesus Culture and began to travel full time.

I had no idea what I was doing then, and still don't know
what I'm doing now. I have learned a lot but consider myself
an expert in nothing. Don't misunderstand me. I am in no way
trying to put myself down or diminish my experience. I simply

want to be honest about the fact that if we think we have "arrived" in any area of our lives, we are probably deceived.

In Christianity there is no "arriving," we are seekers forever in a kingdom without end. You will never know all there is to know, and you will only find what God Himself desires to reveal to you when He reveals it. It's why you can read the same passage of Scripture hundreds of times and then suddenly, years later, wake up and find yourself broken before the same words because your eyes were opened to something you had never seen before.

I had married the woman of my dreams but I was absolutely clueless as to how to care for her heart and steward her deepest desires. I knew how to take care of myself. I knew how to be driven and focused and passionate. I knew how to run after all the dreams and prophetic words I had received over the course of twelve years of ministry. But what I failed to realize is that without humility and love, the same things that cause a man to be great can drive him to arrogance and control even without his own knowledge.

I awoke the morning after we led our set in Chicago, and my wife and I headed to a restaurant in the lobby of our hotel to meet with a friend and spiritual father, Kris Vallotton, from Bethel Church in Redding. The goal of our meeting was to talk about the communication in our marriage and to catch up on how things were going. Little did I know, God had other plans.

Love Demands Confrontation

Our one-hour breakfast turned into a six-hour meeting in Kris's hotel room. Just two weeks shy of our ninth wedding anniversary, my wife, broken hearted and weeping, was telling Kris that she was done with me and what we called a marriage. She was not seeking a divorce and there were no moral failures on either side. The deep chasm between our two hearts had grown so vast. The intimacy and trust my wife longed for had suffered so many disappointments that it was now beyond repair.

It wasn't that she hadn't tried to communicate it. Over the years she had described her broken heart in depth with tears and sadness, but because of the veil over my own eyes and the selfish condition of my heart, I could not hear a single word. Now here in front of a father that she loved and trusted, she jumped out of the boat. She made it quite clear where she was, and that she did not desire for me to fix it or even attempt to come get her.

The craziest part of that meeting was that in the midst of the onslaught of emotion and raw honesty from my wife, I remember thanking God for Kris and for this opportunity to see the wounds I had inflicted, so that we could begin the process of healing. In the moment it didn't seem like some great revelation or deep wisdom. It was a simple fact: *If this doesn't come out and I am not confronted with my own depravity and my own brokenness through the lens of someone who loves me, then I can never change and our marriage won't be saved.*

After Kris had given us some amazing insight and helped remove the veil from my eyes, we went back to our room where I began to realize the extent of the damage I had done to my beautiful bride. She was finally pushing back against what had hurt her for so long, and I had the choice to either sit there and take it, or run away. I wept harder than I had ever wept before. The next day, we drove to the airport with our band. I drove in complete silence while she carried on a friendly conversation pretending nothing had happened. There was more silence on the plane ride and then the drive home from the airport. The silence was only broken by the excitement of our children who had missed their mom and dad. On the exterior I was holding it together, while on the inside I was dying.

Awakened To My Own Depravity

That night after the kids went to bed, the silence was interrupted by hours of tears. I couldn't eat or sleep for days. I was consumed by my own arrogance and overwhelmed by the hurt I had inflicted on my family by forcing them to live around my own selfish lifestyle.

I had become an angry and frustrated person consumed by delusions of grandeur, devoted to my own dreams. I was no fun to be around; I had created an unhealthy environment where fear and control had become necessary tools to carry out my agenda. I may not have hit with my hands, but I definitely took some shots with my words and my actions. Everything I did seemed to shove my family further away; everything communicated that my calling and ministry was more important than their hearts and needs. It was as if I was seeing it for the first time. Layer upon layer of my deception and vanity was being removed.

But God wanted to go deeper, and I was finally in a place to receive what He had been trying to tell me for years. I knew where I needed to look, but it seemed so elementary.

The Fullness of Love

God drew me to 1 Corinthians 13. I had heard that passage for years. It was such a common reading at weddings that by now they seemed empty and corny. But in that moment, the words cut through me—like a knife performing surgery on the deepest hurts inside my own life—and exposed me for who I really was.

Love is patient, love is kind. —1 Corinthians 13:4

It struck me like the bell in a clock tower, ringing through my entire body and shaking me to my core. It felt like all of heaven was yelling, "Slow down and be nice!" It was about one in the morning when I started reading, and I couldn't get past that one line for over three days. This was not an in-depth, hermeneutical exegesis on 1 Corinthians; it was a wakeup call to a thirty-two year old man who was losing what he cared about most.

For years I had pursued my own dreams, leaving those I loved the most in the dust of my schedule and ministry pursuits. Let me tell you, if you don't think you are capable of the same thing, you are already deceived. Any of us is capable of seeking our own agenda at the expense of those around us. It happens with the best of intentions and the poorest of execution.

There is no trace of malice in our hearts when we begin. We all simply run the race set before us, pursuing what we believe is our calling, yet we leave a wake of broken hearts and abandoned people behind us as we search for affirmation and approval. All the while, the people who chose to love us through the good and the bad are left sitting on the sidelines of our lives with our empty promises and what remains of their shattered dreams.

Before we know it, we have made our calling our identity. To slow down or even stop would not only mean the loss of a title, or possibly an income, it would be the loss of who we think we are and how we relate to the world around us. We view the world through the lens of worldly success and call it *kingdom* to justify our barren hearts and broken homes.

I had done this to my own family for nine years. I put my platform and what I believed to be my destiny before my family, and the invitations from the world became more important than the invitation I had into the hearts of my wife and my children.

It was time to slow down.

Be Still and Know

I had to make a choice, a real choice. Would I justify my schedule and ignore the fractured state of my marriage, or would I turn towards home and win back the heart of my bride?

Immaturity would say that you could do both.

Wisdom says there are only so many hours in a day and love takes time. This would require the help of fathers and mothers in my life as well as close friends without agendas.

I tend to be "black and white" with everything I do. I am either all-in or all-out, and neither extreme works when you're dealing with major life changes. I had to put together a schedule that would honor my wife and support our home as the priority of my life. I needed a schedule that would allow God to use me in whatever way He chose while establishing healthy boundaries—boundaries that put God, family, and calling into their proper places.

Ministry and serving God are not the same things as slowing down and loving God. If you spend sixty hours a week in your office meeting with people, flying on planes, or standing on a platform, yet only a few hours sitting in silence and listening to the voice of the Father, you will end up dry and detached from the God you claim to love. We end up learning all the right words and the right actions without ever learning how to love. This is why marriages fail and ministers fall. They focus on what gives them the most satisfaction and call that thing "love" in order to justify a complete lack of intimacy. How can you know the one you love if you have no time to listen to the desires of their heart?

Did you read that last line and think, "Well then, who is supposed to care about my dreams and listen to the desires of my heart?" If so, you are already headed down the wrong path. When God becomes your source of encouragement, comfort, and strength, you stop using applause from man as a crutch for your ego and the compliments of strangers as a bandage for rejection. You will begin to sacrifice all that you have and all that you are for others in a way that shows the world we really are His disciples.

Learning to "Be Nice"

Love requires more than just slowing down. It also requires kindness. The amazing thing about slowing down is that each situation and every circumstance becomes more manageable. There is a greater awareness of your surroundings that allows you to *respond* instead of *react*. The beauty of this is made clear in Romans 2:4 (NASB):

The kindness of God leads you to repentance.

When we have slowed down enough to survey the current landscape of our lives with the Holy Spirit, we can show kindness to others who hurt us and allow them to see the error in their ways without ever addressing it. God's response to our arrogance and rebellion is to offer up His life in exchange for ours. The cross is God's way of saying, "I don't care how much you have done or how much you will do. I am laying down my life for you. It's your lack, not your perfection, that demands my attention and requires my sacrifice."

God recognizes our needs and the depth of our sin more than we will ever understand in this life. In the midst of what C.S. Lewis coined "the great divorce," God makes a way for us to come near to Him while we are still beating on His chest, frustrated and immature. That great kindness is the most beautiful display of love in human history—it is that great kindness, extended to us, that will change the world.

But how is it that God can love like that? One word: *Perspective.*

God sees all eternity as an eternal present. He is the God of "now." The "now" of fifty years ago and the "now" five thousand years in the future are the same to God. Therefore, every action and reaction from humanity doesn't shake, scare, or distract God from His goals. He knows that He has the ability to work all things to the good of those who love Him (Romans 8:28) because He has years and years to work out what we get frustrated about in ten minutes.

We want to be a raging inferno, yet God is looking for those who will burn slow and steady. The feeling that we must get everything done today leads us to create personality-driven ministries that are directed by pet doctrines. It leads us to protect our ministries at the expense of the people.

Sound doctrine is not our first priority, love is. Love will lead us to sound doctrine and great depths of intimacy that will sustain us through every trial and every testing. If we refuse to grasp the truth of patient endurance—what the Bible calls "long-suffering"—we will spend a lifetime attempting to lead others to be like *us* instead of Jesus.

My wife asked me for years to simply be nice. Why couldn't I just answer her request? I kept wondering why I was so short with her and the kids. I would get frustrated simply at the fact that I was getting frustrated. It became an endless cycle of ups and downs, highs and lows. Abrasiveness became my hallmark. Nobody wants to hang out with a guy who gets frustrated and ruins everybody's day simply because something didn't go the way he expected. Does any day ever go perfectly according to plan anyway? No.

As I was reading the simple passage from 1 Corinthians 13, I realized that what I needed more than another round of counseling or deliverance was to slow down. I simply needed to remove things from my schedule, give myself more time to get to places, and give myself more than just a few hours to get a week's worth of work done. If I succeeded in these small efforts, I could alleviate the pressure of performance and give myself the ability to enjoy each moment of my life, rather than simply reacting to what got in my way.

Love was starting to take on life for me.

This wasn't just a list of demands found in the Bible to condemn the way I had been acting. It was a breath of fresh air into the lungs of a man drowning in his own selfish nature. All this revelation was just from the first two attributes in a list of sixteen!

Living a Lifestyle of Love

This passage is calling a generation into a lifestyle modeled by Jesus and displayed by those who know Him as Lord, Savior, and Friend. These words in 1 Corinthians 13:4-7 are not just adjectives describing what love looks like. They are all verbs in the original Greek language describing the active and dynamic lifestyle of those deliberately seeking to glorify Christ in every aspect of their existence.

You cannot master the behaviors described in 1 Corinthians in one day. It is a life-long journey guided by the Holy Spirit and consummated by Jesus Christ. This passage is more than a hymn to the beauty of love or a description of love that only God Himself is capable of. This section of Scripture is integral to the teaching of Paul to the Corinthian church on how to live a life possessed by the Holy Spirit, displaying the kingdom of God.

Paul began his exhortation by saying that tongues, prophecy, miracles, signs and wonders, and even giving are incapable of displaying the majesty and beauty of God in the same way that love can. Although I love all those things and believe in the gifts and all the manifestations of the Holy Spirit, love truly is a more excellent way. It is not better than the gifts; it is the context for their existence.

A More Excellent Way

Love does not envy. It is content in every circumstance and every situation. Whether in poverty or in plenty, we can find peace and confidence. There is a beauty that is revealed when we learn to blow in the wind and ride on the tides of normal, everyday life. We cannot be moved by every high and low in our lives and allow them to dictate our emotional and spiritual well-being. We cannot look at others and wish we could obtain what they possess. To be content means that I have the ability to grow wherever I am planted. No matter what transitions, trials, or tests lie ahead, I will not base my happiness or my ability to love on the blessings I find in others' lives. God knows where to place me so that I can grow into the person He designed me to be before time began.

Love does not boast. It does not speak out of turn or flaunt the blessings it has in the face of others. We have earned nothing and are deserving of nothing. Every day and every breath are a gift from God. Love knows how to remain silent in the face of accusation and does not show off in the company of those who are less fortunate.

Love is not arrogant but walks in humility. It allows you to consider others as more important than yourself (Philippians 2:3). Love allows you to call out the identity in others without any cost to your own identity. Love always chooses the low road and champions the dreams and visions of others first, considering others more valuable than yourself.

Love is never rude or impolite. It always takes into consideration the feelings of someone else before it speaks. True words from the Father's heart sometimes involve more than just the right information; they also require gentleness and sensitivity. Just because something is "right" does not make it "truth." We do not know the whole story of someone's heart or the motivations from which they are acting. The Father's love takes a person's past and experiences into consideration and always desires to protect the other's heart before speaking. I believe sarcasm is the passive form of rudeness and should not be tolerated in the Body of Christ. We cannot afford to give ourselves to language that places humor above the encouragement of our brothers and sisters.

Love does not demand its own way or seek itself. Love does not say, "I love you," just so it can hear it in return. It needs no response and requires no recourse to get its approval. It finds its fullness in and of itself and asks nothing in return. Love is completely unconditional.

Love is not irritable, annoyed, or frustrated. It doesn't react to situations or circumstances with anger when things don't go according to plan.

Love keeps no record of wrongs. There is no logbook of ways people have mistreated you in which you hope to pay them back one day. Love does not ignore evil; love simply absorbs hurt without any intention to retaliate.

Love does not rejoice in wrongdoing. It finds no pleasure in the failure of others and it never says, "I told you so."

Love rejoices with the truth. It rejoices no matter how uncomfortable it may be. Sometimes there are things we need to hear even if we do not want to hear them. Proverbs 27:6 (NASB) promises us,

> Faithful are the wounds of a friend, but deceitful are the kisses of an enemy.

Love builds up even while correcting.

Love always protects the one it beholds. The lover always jumps to serve the beloved, even at the cost of their own safety, goals, and dreams. There is never a price too great or cost too high for the one who loves.

Love believes all things. This is not an encouragement to an over-imaginative, gullible, or blind love. This love always puts its full confidence in the one it loves, even when it has been let down. It never demands perfection before it responds. Its ability to see the greatness in the one it loves draws the beloved to become that which the lover sees.

Love finds hope in all circumstances. Love allows an individual to prophesy the future with clarity and peace and without condemnation. If faith is being sure of what we hope for, then love is the fuel that sets fire to our faith. In love we see the best in all things without the need to tear others down or live in the constant anxiety of what might be or should have been.

Love endures through all things. To win in the Christian life, all you have to do is never give up. That's it. Don't quit and you win. Everyone wants breakthrough, but nobody wants to run into anything. When everything around you looks like it is falling apart, love allows you to smile and move forward. How is that possible? It's the reality that you are loved despite every failure and every shortcoming even when life seems to have gotten the best of you.

You are loved. That's where real salvation begins and ends. We are the targets of God's love. His love fulfills all the attributes in this list so perfectly that, when it was walked out on earth in the form of Jesus Christ, it was an offense to many. When false love is confronted by true love, there is only one option: kill it. False love desires to kill the truth and beauty of real love because if it doesn't, it will have to live at the same standard in order to make its voice heard again.

If you attempt to kill love in order to protect your platform or position, consider this first:

Love never fails. You can beat it, yell at it, stab it, tear at it, crucify it, bury it in the ground, and guard it with professional soldiers, but love always finds a way. Real love can never be hindered, even in death. That's the beauty of the Christian message: love never dies and never shrinks back. Love never runs away or pushes you away. Love makes no demands, seeks no control. Love's only aim is freedom. It's beyond emotion, beyond comprehension, beyond conventionality, and beyond the reach of manipulation. Love cannot be purchased and it is impossible to sell.

Love is a man, and His name is Jesus. There is no greater display of love and kindness in all of human history. He saw us at our most broken, fragile, and sinful point and chose love instead of judgment. He took the death we deserved and gave us life. The question is whether or not we will do the same for others.

It's Time to Make Covenant

It took five days of weeping, praying, and fasting before I saw the door of my wife's heart open again. There were five long, empty, gut-wrenching nights where I was unsure if there was any future for my marriage beyond the cordial agreements made by two individuals who had now drifted apart. But I was unwilling to let go; I was unwilling to turn aside from the love of my life, the most beautiful woman I have ever met and the mother of my children. I refused to partner with despair and depression and forced myself to move forward, completely in the hope that love would not fail.

I poured my heart out to my wife each day through tears and repentance but she had heard it all before. It was going to take real change in order to win her heart and it was going to take time. But I did not sign up to be married as long as it was easy. Rather, I was in for the long haul and I was not going anywhere. I have told my wife several times, and I have said it publicly, that if she were to cheat on me and leave me for another, I would remain faithful and pursue her until the day I die.

Although I know that she'd never be unfaithful, I had to learn to love in such a way that if I experienced the most grievous betrayal, I would love in the same way that my Creator has loved me. We are the Bride, and the one true husband of the Church, Jesus Christ, does not turn away when we are unfaithful or pursue other lovers. I want to love like that. The scary thing is that true love allows for the freedom to reject that love. Real freedom is not found in the abundance of choices, but in the beauty of one choice forever. That's what covenant is all about.

Covenant is an agreement between two parties that no matter what happens, we are together. Whether that choice takes us to the pits of despair or the heights of greatness, we are committed forever. This is the glorious beauty found in the covenant of marriage. You will never again have to wonder if someone cares, if someone will be there for you, if someone is thinking about you, or if someone has your best interest in mind. We must defend the covenants we have made in our lives, beginning with the most precious covenant we will make on earth outside of our covenant with Jesus: our marriage.

The covenant of marriage is the greatest model of the kingdom of heaven on earth. Greater than any sign and wonder you
will ever see is a marriage that has lasted fifty, sixty, or seventy
years. Marriage is a daily choice to die to yourself so that you
have an opportunity to serve the heart and dreams of another in
tangible, practical ways.

Love really does look like something. Our greatest teachers
are the circumstances and situations God allows in the context
of our marriages to form humility and generosity in ways that
cannot be formed in any other environment. At its foundation,
love is about giving not receiving. If we refuse this truth, we will
make love a selfish pursuit for vanity and leave broken hearts in
the wake of our arrogant choices.

Maybe you are reading this as a single person and are thinking, "This has nothing to do with me." Wrong. It has everything
to do with you. If you have an understanding of what I am sharing with you, you will be able to save yourself from heartache
and make better choices than so many who have gone before
you. You must stop pursuing marriage or your next relationship
from the fear of being alone. When God looked at Adam in the
Garden of Eden, He recognized that it was not good for man to
be alone. God has a plan for you. He knows what's best for you
(Jeremiah 29:11). He loves you more than anyone you will encounter here on earth. Slow down and enjoy the process of being
formed into His image. When the timing is right, you will be
prepared to love in a way that will help your marriage last and go
deeper than you could have ever hoped. Please heed the warning
from Song of Songs 8:4 (NLT):

[Do not] awaken love before the time is right.

Pursuing "One Thing"

Love looks like something, but love is so much more than just serving or works. Look at the story of Martha and Mary from Luke 10. Jesus is found in the company of two young ladies and their brother, Lazarus, relaxing and sharing His heart in their home. Martha, the eldest sister, takes a brief departure from her household duties to demand that Jesus tell her younger sister, Mary, to get up and help her. Jesus' response was a strong rebuke against the lifestyle Martha had chosen. He told her that she was distracted by many things and that Mary had found the one good thing.

Sometimes in our attempt to love out of our insecurity and rejection, we try to serve others to prove our love is real. Unless we get past this, we will never attain any depth with those we love the most. It was Mary who found something Jesus was excited about. He said that Mary had found the one good thing and it would not be taken from her.

> As Jesus and his disciples were on their way, he came to a village where a woman named Martha opened her home to him. She had a sister called Mary, **who sat at the Lord's feet listening to what he said**. But Martha was distracted by all the preparations that had to be made. She came to him and asked, "Lord, don't you care that my sister has left me to do the work by myself? Tell her to help me!"
>
> "Martha, Martha," the Lord answered, "you are worried and upset about many things, but few things

are needed—or indeed only one. Mary has chosen what is better, and it will not be taken away from her."

—Luke 10:38-42

Mary slowed down and listened to every word that came from His mouth. This is the simplicity of life that Jesus not only blesses but defends. He is not looking for someone with a good performance record or perfect attendance. He is looking for a heart that is fully devoted to Him so He can strengthen, equip, and empower them from on high.

Going unnoticed on earth is okay if you're recognized by heaven. A young girl sitting at His feet was far greater than anything else He could have been offered in that house. He wasn't looking for funding; He wasn't interested in a platform. He wasn't even looking for food or shelter. He wanted their *attention* and *affection*, and that is all He wants today.

I recognize that isn't glamorous.

It was never meant to be.

Love is a call to walk in humility while serving others and dying to yourself. Through this, you will be able to find what truly matters.

Once You Find Love, Never Let It Go

Today my marriage is better than it has ever been! God Himself broke into two human hearts and gave us the grace to see each other and our covenant in the same way He sees it. We desperately need the Holy Spirit to lead us and be our advocate in the face of our accuser as we discover true love and learn how to walk in it. That is all it took for us. The possibility of losing everything was the wakeup call we needed.

If you are married, I challenge you to turn your heart towards home and ask a dangerous question to your spouse, "What do you need from me that I am not currently giving?" When your spouse answers you, do not get upset or frustrated or try to justify yourself. Simply ask God to tear the veil from your eyes so you can see and feel it from their perspective. At that point you have a choice: are you going to go low and serve the request of your spouse, or will you continue without change? With the power of the Holy Spirit in your life, I know you will do it because love does not seek its own. Real love says, "I can serve you without need of anything in return. I love you with open hands and an open heart."

If you are not married, you have an opportunity to build habits today that will protect your future marriage and fuel intimacy. Make the priority of your life listening and responding to the Holy Spirit. Remember that the will of God for every human being is the same:

> "Love the Lord your God with all your heart and with all your soul and with all your strength and with all your mind." —Luke 10:27

This is what God is looking for from your life. Are you doing it? Is the priority of your life to slow down and make time for what really matters? Or is your goal to speed up and have the appearance of success? What good are degrees and a big house if you are empty inside? Jesus said,

> "What good is it for someone to gain the whole world, yet forfeit their soul?" —Mark 8:36

Heaven doesn't need performers or promoters. It is time to lay down your life for love, for by this everyone will know that you are a disciple of Jesus: "if you love one another" (John 13:35).

ABOUT THE AUTHOR: Jake Hamilton is a passionate worshiper carrying the language and sound of reformation. He has a deep desire to see generational and denominational boundaries blurred through the simple message of love embodied in the man Jesus Christ and lived out in the context of community. As an artist, he desires to push the limits of creativity. As a father and a husband, he is committed to his family first. But above all his endorsements and accomplishments, he is a lover of Jesus Christ with the ability to lead others into the same encounter that has transformed his life since 1997. He has been a part of Jesus Culture Music since 2009, while leading worship and preaching around the world. To find out more information on the ministry of Jake Hamilton or to book Jake for an event please visit www.jakehamiltonmusic.com.

SIX

❖

The Unoffendable Heart

By Brian Brennt

Ten years ago my wife, Christy, had an amazing dream. In this dream, Christy was sitting in the audience of a game show called "Insult." One by one, the contestants were brought up on the stage to receive a barrage of personal insults crafted just for them. The contestants survived the early rounds of the game, but eventually each broke down and started shouting insults back at the judges. Christy was called to the stage and the host and his team yelled every insult they could at her. But with every word, Christy simply smiled and spoke grace, diffusing the entire team. She was unable to be offended. Finally the host and team threw their arms in the air and laughed. Christy had won the grand prize! Never before had someone won the grand prize. At the end of the dream, the Holy Spirit whispered, "I am going to work in you to fulfill the dream." This dream served as a blueprint for us as we embarked on a course of discovery of the "unoffendable" heart.

We often talk about forgiveness in generic terms. It's easy to say you've forgiven someone without actually addressing the offense that you feel. I wanted to forgive people and walk in the unoffendable heart, but the problem was I could not figure out very easily if I had become offended. I did a general forgiveness prayer and tried to move on, but offense had gotten in under my radar and was stealing from me the freshness of walking with Jesus.

As I pursued this understanding, the first thing God revealed to me was that our hearts are like dashboards in a car. There are four key indicator lights that show us if we are offended or are holding a grudge against someone. When these warning lights flash, we can know that offense has taken hold in our hearts.

Indicator One: Dwelling on your Offense

Do you ever find yourself replaying conversations in your head? Do you imagine what you would say to the person who offended you? Perhaps you think of all the ways you can tell them off or set them straight. These conversations may go beyond staying in your head—you might share your negative thoughts with other people. Either way, you are still dwelling on the person or situation.

I remember taking a shower one time and suddenly blurting out something negative about a person who offended me. My oldest son Nick, who was about ten years old at the time, knocked on the bathroom door and asked me whom I was talking to. That was an amazing revelation. The bitterness indicator light was flashing in my heart. It was time to identify what I needed to forgive and actively pursue the unoffendable heart.

Indicator Two: Avoiding the Person who Offended You

There is no mystery here. Who are you avoiding and why? We all have those people in our lives that seem to carry the "party crasher" anointing. It seems that right when something amazing has just happened, the party crasher finds me and either tells me bad news or makes sure I remember my character flaws and struggles. Or perhaps the party crasher is a person who was critical of you, gossiped, or withheld encouragement from you when you needed it the most. It could be a person who betrayed your confidence or rejected you.

Regardless of the offense, the point the Holy Spirit was bringing up with me was simply this: *You have become offended and you need to quickly forgive and embrace the people around you with love.* I realized that I had only forgiven the person who offended me in principle, but not from a heart of love.

Indicator Three: Being Critical of the Person who Offended You

Job 16:4-5 (NLT) gets right to the point:

> I could say the same things if you were in my place. I could spout off my criticisms against you and shake my head at you. But that's not what I would do. I would speak in a way that helps you. I would try to take away your grief.

A critical, offended heart regards people and circumstances from a negative point of view. The offended heart is impatient, irritable, unforgiving, unbending, and ungrateful. It struggles with anger and bitterness.

The Holy Spirit began to show me that an offended heart is a critical heart, and when the dashboard light of criticism was blinking, I needed to pull the car over and get my heart in order.

The work of a critical spirit includes the following:

- Creates a negative, sour, judgmental, and repressive atmosphere
- Points out the weaknesses, idiosyncrasies, and inconsistencies of others with a view to tearing them down instead of building them up
- Criticizes family, friends, co-workers, and members of the church family without bringing solutions, encouragement, or positive motivation
- Quenches vision, creativity, unity, and teamwork

When the dash light of criticism is blinking, then you know you have entered the offended-heart zone. Ask yourself these simple questions to get back on track:

- Whom am I speaking critically about?
- Am I pointing out the weaknesses of others or highlighting their strengths?
- Am I championing the dreams of others?

Once you identify what is happening in your heart, the steps are clear. Humble yourself and get every ounce of offense out of your heart. Forgive people from the depth of your heart, and begin to speak and demonstrate love about every person you have been critical of.

The Bible is filled with all kinds of incredible instructions about the unoffendable heart. Read through each of these verses slowly and soak in the truth of how we are to treat one another.

He who covers over an offense promotes love, but whoever repeats the matter separates close friends.

—Proverbs 17:9

"Do not judge, or you too will be judged. For in the same way you judge others, you will be judged, and with the measure you use, it will be measured to you."

—Matthew 7:1-2

"Why do you look at the speck of sawdust in your brother's eye and pay no attention to the plank in your own eye? How can you say to your brother, 'Let me take the speck out of your eye,' when all the time there is a plank in your own eye? You hypocrite, first take the plank out of your own eye, and then you will see clearly to remove the speck from your brother's eye." —Matthew 7:3-5

"Do not judge, and you will not be judged. Do not condemn, and you will not be condemned. Forgive, and you will be forgiven." —Luke 6:37

You, then, why do you judge your brother? Or why do you look down on your brother? For we will all stand before God's judgment seat. It is written: "As surely as I live," says the Lord, "every knee will bow before me; every tongue will confess to God." So then, each of us will give an account of himself to God. Therefore let us stop passing judgment on one another. Instead, make up your mind not to put any stumbling block or obstacle in your brother's way.

—Romans 14:10-13

We who are strong ought to bear with the failings of the weak and not to please ourselves. —Romans 15:1

Brothers, if someone is caught in a sin, you who are spiritual should restore him gently. But watch yourself, or you also may be tempted. Carry each other's burdens, and in this way you will fulfill the law of Christ. If anyone thinks he is something when he is nothing, he deceives himself. Each one should test his own actions. Then he can take pride in himself, without comparing himself to somebody else. —Galatians 6:1-4

Bear with each other and forgive whatever grievances you may have against one another. Forgive as the Lord forgave you. And over all these virtues put on love, which binds them all together in perfect unity.

—Colossians 3:13-14

Speak and act as those who are going to be judged by the law that gives freedom, because judgment without mercy will be shown to anyone who has not been merciful. Mercy triumphs over judgment.

—James 2:12-13

Indicator Four: Becoming a Diagnostic Expert on How Everyone Should Live Their Life

This indicator light spoke volumes about where my heart was. We have all been around an "opinion master" who knows exactly what everyone around them needs to be doing. If you are with an opinion master, you know it is like being with a full-time movie critic. But instead of critiquing movies, they criticize people, churches, organizations, families, and schools. In other words, nothing is out of their realm of expertise.

I remember visiting a church in my twenties in full movie-critic mode. I had never led more than a small Bible study, but that did not stop me from evaluating every moment of the service. I am sure the pastor could see a small cloud of gloom over my section as my mind raced with every way things *really* needed to be done.

In my "discernment," I decided that the man giving announcements was way too happy, the people were fake, and nobody was worshipping God the right way. Even the message was not deep enough for me—I needed the "ultimate message." The car ride home was the perfect time for me to bring all of my insights up about how things really needed to be run.

The opinion master is not so much offended with others as they are better than others. Pride has entered in and the unoffendable heart has been shelved, at least for now. Pride can be defined as having an overly high opinion of oneself. As I read the Scriptures below, I began to write down the opposite spirit of pride and the offended heart. As I began to declare with my heart and actions the heart of God, I felt Him tenderizing my heart and moving me forward in every action.

> When pride comes, then comes disgrace, but with humility comes wisdom. —Proverbs 11:2

> You rescue those who are humble, but you humiliate the proud. —Psalm 18:27 (NLT)

> He guides the humble in what is right and teaches them his way. —Psalm 25:9

> To fear the LORD is to hate evil; I hate pride and arrogance, evil behavior and perverse speech.
> —Proverbs 8:13

As the Bible aligned my heart back into unoffendable mode, I found myself totally filled with fresh joy and love, not only for the people around me, but also for myself. It's a sad truth that the most critical people also struggle with self-criticism. We treat others the way we treat ourselves. I not only needed to love others, but I needed to love myself. As all of this came to light, it seemed almost too good to be true. The opinion master was going into retirement and in his place was the unoffendable heart.

Creating a Lifestyle of Grace

Cultivating an unoffendable heart creates a lifestyle of grace towards others. A grateful heart and selfless servant will always put others first. But what does this mean in practice? The following encouragements have helped me understand just what it means to cultivate an unoffendable heart. These statements became prayers for me, and God began to build these into my everyday life. Make them your prayer as you read them now.

- I will be patient and forbearing toward the weaknesses of others.
- I will guard myself against speaking critically about anyone at any time.
- I will not take or carry offenses for myself or for others.
- When there is a need to discuss differences, I will communicate in humility and speak the truth in love.
- I will offer my opinions only when asked, or under the direction of the Holy Spirit.
- I will lead others in an understanding and patient manner.
- When someone accuses or criticizes me, I will respond with humility and an open mind; I will not respond defensively.
- When I feel someone is attacking me personally, I will choose to look at the situation through spiritual eyes, being on the alert for schemes of the enemy.
- I will make it a high priority to preserve unity with my family, friends, church, community, and anyone else God brings into my life.

The unoffendable heart is a heart of forgiveness lived out. It says, "No matter what happens, I am going to forgive." Paul explains to us the posture, or attitude, that forgiveness comes from.

And be kind to one another, tenderhearted, forgiving
each other, just as God in Christ also has forgiven
you. —Ephesians 4:32 (NASB)

God asks us to treat one another with kindness and tender-
ness. We can pour out forgiveness to each other because Jesus
has forgiven each of us.

The end of a matter is better than its beginning;
Patience of spirit is better than haughtiness of spirit.
Do not be eager in your heart to be angry, For anger
resides in the bosom of fools. Do not say, "Why is it
that the former days were better than these?" For it is
not from wisdom that you ask about this.
                    —Ecclesiastes 7:8-10 (NASB)

The Bible tells us that "anger resides in the bosom of fools"
(Ecclesiastes 7:9). Unforgiveness creates resentment, anger, hatred, and emotional damage. Paul traces the development of unresolved bitterness in Ephesians 4:31. Bitterness leads to wrath,
wrath leads to anger, and anger leads to clamor (making a public
scene). Clamor is followed by slander, and slander leads to malice
(inner hatred of the heart). The danger of harboring an attitude
of bitterness is that eventually it will control you.

Paul warns that bitterness is like a root. The longer it is al-
lowed to grow, the more difficult it is to dig it out. Hebrews 12:15
states that a root of bitterness left to grow will bring defilement
to *many*. The root will produce the fruit of anger, ungratefulness,
a critical attitude, insensitivity to others, revenge, mistrust, and
depression. Unresolved bitterness is also like a highly contagious
disease with a contaminating and destructive effect on others.

The cure for bitterness and anger is forgiveness. In order to resolve bitterness, we must first understand and experience God's forgiveness of our sin. God chose to focus on His desire to forgive us rather than to hold us accountable for our failures (Isaiah 43:25; 55:7; Psalm 103:12).

Forgiveness demands a payment. When someone has sinned against us and hurt us, our sense of justice demands that a fair payment be made to us for their failure, whether it is in the physical, mental, emotional, or spiritual arena. If that person cannot pay back what we think they owe, or willfully chooses not to pay, we can either resent the injustice and become bitter and angry, or we can exercise forgiveness, which leads to peace. Forgiveness is not excusing or dismissing the sin. Forgiveness is fully acknowledging the sin did happen and that it was hurtful and wrong, but then we give our right to execute justice over to God so He can handle it in His way and in His time.

Forgiveness is not easy, especially when something has caused us great harm or damage. However, as we free the offender through forgiveness, we free ourselves from the effects of holding onto destructive attitudes.

Let's take a few moments to go through a checklist to identify areas of unforgiveness, bitterness, or anger that may need to be resolved in your life. One indicator of whether or not true forgiveness has occurred is your ability, through the Holy Spirit, to pray a powerful blessing on a person who has hurt you.

Have You Been Hurt in One or More of These Areas?

- Control/manipulation
- Neglect

- Abandonment
- Rejection
- Criticism
- Performance-based acceptance and love
- Alcohol abuse
- Drug use
- Pornography
- Adultery
- Divorce
- Withholding affection
- Withholding blessing
- Withholding words of encouragement
- Withholding discipline
- Other ways you have been hurt

The items checked on the preceding list need to be brought to the cross. Talk to God about these hurts using a prayer like I have given below.

> Lord Jesus, I forgive _____ *(person who hurt you)* for the sin of _____ *(list here all of the sins for which you need to forgive the person).* Lord Jesus, I ask You to forgive me for the sin of unforgiveness toward _____ for these sins. Forgive me for bitterness, resentment, and anger toward _____.

Jesus, I now want to pray a blessing on _____. *(Stand up to pray this prayer. Pray with all of your heart and strength; raise your voice and pray with faith.)*

I pray that You would:

- Bless _____ with salvation.
- Bless _____ with the same freedom I have found today.
- Bless _____ with a new and soft heart.
- Bless _____ with a strong and fruitful marriage.
- Bless _____'s finances and work.
- Bless _____ with joy, peace, kindness, love, and all of the fruit of the Spirit.

I declare that I love _____ with the love that Christ has loved me. I declare that _____ is Your child.

I ask in faith that You would pour Your love on _____. Do it now, Lord. My chains are broken and I stand free before You. Thank You for the power of the cross.

Renounce and Rebuke

Stand up and pray the following prayer with conviction, with all of your heart, and with faith that God will move in a powerful way right now.

> Jesus, I now renounce a life of anger, bitterness, and unforgiveness. I renounce the right to take offense. I give up my right to see justice. I give You this relationship with _____, and it is in Your hands now. I am not responsible for things that only You can do. I cut that cord now.

Replace

When thoughts of bitterness occur, rebuke them and replace them with thoughts of blessing. Stand firm—don't take up offense again.

The culture of the unoffendable heart is one of the greatest joys you could ever have. It will not always be easy to maintain, but being motivated by what Jesus has done for you will give you the strength to arise and live with a tenderized heart before Him.

ABOUT THE AUTHOR: Brian Brennt and his wife, Christy, have a call of God on their lives to awaken, prepare, and see revival break out in America and ripple across the world. They are passionate soul winners who carry the message of the gospel everywhere they go. They are firmly believing God for the mobilization of a massive wave of missionaries out of America. Forged through the place of intercession and brokenness, their entire family carries the same burden for revival. Brian is a graduate of Faith Seminary where he earned a Doctorate in Leadership. The beginning days of Brian and Christy's ministry came out of an outbreak of salvation and repentance in Tacoma, Washington. They function often as a team and are filled with the joy that can only come from spending time together in the place of prayer. Their children are Nick (20), Chloe (18), Spencer (16), and Joshua (10). To contact Brian and Christy, or to order their books (*The Freedom Manual, Big 10 – Truth Encounters,* and *Salvation Encounter*), e-mail them at salvationencounter@gmail.com.

✵

SEVEN

Activation from Habitation

By Sean Feucht

It all begins with intimacy.

Intimacy is not just a piece of this culture—another thing to check off the list—but it is the very ignition point of the entire movement. It is our "once upon a time" fairy tale opening line. It plays out something like this:

> *Once upon a time, a generation was obsessively and radically in love with a man named Jesus. From this place of profound and abandoned love, they brought God's kingdom to earth and lived happily ever after. The end.*

God's kingdom of revival, transformation, signs, and wonders only comes through deep and sustained love for the presence of God. Intimacy is the glue that holds the story together. It is the oil that allows the engine of revival to function, preventing it from burning out. It is the rock solid foundation the revival culture house is built upon. Without this sure and steadfast foundation of intimacy, when the storms of life kick up their gusts, even our great disciplines—values, anointings, and formulas—will not be enough to withstand it. We must be rooted in the place of fiery first love!

Strong Love

We need a fresh baptism of intimacy and love that is stronger than temptations, sufferings, and even death. This love is the foundation that every significant revival in history has stood on since the fiery upper room of Acts 2. If love is neglected or placed as an afterthought, revival will abruptly come to an end.

Matthew 24 records Jesus describing the events of the last days. He speaks of things that ring loud and clear to us today. He tells of earthquakes, floods, famines, and darkness that will cover the earth. Wars and rumors of wars will break out as "nation rises against nation" (verse 7). The kicker comes when He ties the increase of wickedness and disillusionment to the loss of first love.

> "Because of the increase of wickedness, the love of most will grow cold, but he who stands firm to the end will be saved." —Matthew 24:12–13

Jesus then teaches the disciples how to sustain their love through the dark days of shaking. Through the parable of the ten virgins, He shows us how we must have the oil of intimacy in order to faithfully wait for His return. As the time draws nearer to the return of Christ, the global shakings and widespread uncertainties will increase in strength and quantity. We must be rooted in intimacy, carrying the fresh oil of His presence. We must embody and display strong love in our homes, families, communities, and ministries. This is our first calling before any other calling.

Let this prayer below become the mantra of a generation diving headfirst into a love that grows stronger and stronger with each new day:

> Place me like a seal over your heart, like a seal on your arm; for love is as strong as death, its jealousy unyielding as the grave. It burns like blazing fire, like a mighty flame. Many waters cannot quench love; rivers cannot wash it away. —Song of Songs 8:6-7

The Ancient Path

Establishing a lifestyle and culture of intimacy in our families, communities, and ministries does not require us to reinvent the wheel. Many generations before us have prioritized intimacy and it always led to transformation in personal lives, families, and communities. This journey has been the intention and dream of God since the beginning and will remain our destiny, inheritance, and eternal reward in the end.

We are at a crossroads right now, looking for the way of the ancient paths of sustained delight in His presence. These paths are the "good way" and release much "rest for our souls" (Jeremiah 6:16). In many ways, this is a call to return back to the Garden of Eden. Our original purpose and design was to walk intimately with God in the cool of the day (Genesis 3:6). Intimacy was never supposed to be laborious or cumbersome but as easy as breathing in the breath of God. The garden was created as the perfect backdrop for this divine interaction. Maybe this is why many escape to picturesque mountains, peaceful forests, or shimmering waterfalls to be intimate with God. The longing we feel is rooted deep in our core. We were created for this!

Activation from Habitation

When we look at David on the Judean hillside or John the Baptist in the Qumran wilderness, we see that their moment of ministry activation came through their habitation. Instead of striving or manipulating to fill a ministry position, they were cultivating a heart for His presence. They understood that God alone was their promoter. That is why hanging out with a herd of sheep or a company of fasting prophets (the Essenes) seemed ideal to them. Even though their lives and family heritage were marked by profound prophetic words, they were not eager to force or strong-arm those words into action. They focused on spending time in intimacy with their Father. Their true commissioning came in the wilderness. Through them, God found His next voice to a generation and they experienced the truth of Jesus' words:

> "Remain in me, and I will remain in you. No branch can bear fruit by itself; it must remain in the vine. Neither can you bear fruit unless you remain in me… If a man remains in me and I in him, he will bear much fruit; apart from me you can do nothing."
>
> —John 15:4–5

The life of Jesus is the most profound example of this revelation fully lived out. It also gives us an incredible glimpse into how practical this intimate life can be. Even though Jesus spent years working as a carpenter, He was not simply a gifted or anointed man showered with powerful prophetic words—He was the Son of the living God! He carried the fullness of Almighty God in Him and the power to deliver all mankind from the evil of his ways (let alone heal a next door neighbor or two). Yet, He practiced restraint. As far as we know, He did no public ministry and performed no great signs or wonders in the first thirty years of His life.

Have you ever thought about this before? What in the world was He doing all those years? Didn't He see the corruption of the social, religious, and political leaders? What about the depressed, sick, and dying people all around Him? How about the blind beggars and town lepers? Why didn't He use His power, authority, and strength to heal people or challenge the authorities?

Jesus was not having an identity crisis in these first thirty years. I believe He was moving with the priorities of heaven and closely guarding and protecting the most valuable asset in His life: the cultivation of intimacy with His Father. His mother had to push Him (as mothers do) to launch into ministry on that wedding night in Cana (John 2). It seemed like Jesus was in no hurry.

So what was He doing all that time? I believe He was practically walking out intimacy with every piece of wood He cut, every nail He hammered, and every meal He made. A life of communion and prayer with His Father became incredibly practical and tangibly real. Not basing His relationship on ministry performance, He was perfectly content living life with God during every mundane task or boring day. He dug His well deeper and deeper every day as a dependent Son who later testified that He wanted to "do only what He saw His Father do" (John 5:19). Oh how I wish the eager, hungry, and young revivalists of our generation would grab onto this principle. How it would break off our orphaned and works-oriented approach to the Father.

The Standard Set

If Jesus, being fully the Son of God, chose to spend thirty years hiding away in the secret place, then the standard of intimacy has been set incredibly high for us. We must be fully immersed in the oil of intimacy in order to make the transition from habitation to activation. We do not need any more independent itinerant rock-star ministers, one-man shows, or performance-driven Christianity. Striving in our own strength produces meager results and little fruit. A culture devoid of intimacy will always lead to exhaustion and brokenness.

We cannot afford to lose more gifted and anointed leaders to burnout. If we do not daily drink in the presence of the Lord, we will become like "broken cisterns that cannot hold water" (Jeremiah 2:13). The result almost always ends in blinding pride, family destruction, and a wide-open door to sin and the accuser of the brethren. We need an army of meek, humble, and devout lovers dripping with the oil of intimacy and walking in the true revelation of sonship! We must be completely dependent on every word coming out of our Father's mouth.

This creates a culture of transformation and revival everywhere our feet tread. The world is an overcrowded orphanage overwhelmed with deprived, neglected, and cynical children who are longing to know their real Daddy. Intimacy is what they crave and intimacy is what we must carry.

Eager Expectation

Romans 8:19 declares:

The creation waits in eager expectation for the sons of God to be revealed.

There is an eager expectation brooding in the nations of the world for the true sons and daughters of God to arise! I can feel it every time my plane touches down near the slums of Mumbai, the hipster scene of Seattle, the crowded mosques of Turkey, the island villages of Indonesia, or the halls of Harvard. The people of the world are longing to see the sons of God. They wait with eager expectation to see those who intimately know, carry, and release a revelation of God.

Many young people today are anxious to be activated into full-time ministry without first building a heritage and legacy with God. This always leads to the tragic epidemic taking out a generation of ministers: burnout. God gives the gifts without repentance, but if you try to rely only on your gifts for your success, you will fail.

Think of it like a powerful V8 engine in a muscle car. The engine may be built for great speed and endurance, but if it isn't given motor oil, the engine will eventually grind to a halt and refuse to function. The motor oil works as a lubricant and causes all the parts to work and operate smoothly and with ease. In the same way, your gifts, calling, and anointing only function properly when they are moving with the oil of intimacy with the Holy Spirit. This oil lubricates the engine of our hearts and recalibrates our lives with a grace and ease in His presence. True full-time ministry is all about being full on for God and full of His presence…no matter what you're doing.

The true culture of revival begins with the culture of laid-down lovers in intimacy. This is the bedrock of our communities and the ignition point for all that we do. Like the legendary Moravians, renowned Celts, and the Book of Acts church, we are empowered from the place of intimacy to be joyful witnesses (martyrs) to the ends of the earth (Acts 1:8). Our mandate and commission is to seek intimacy with God no matter where He sends us. We are to seek intimacy with God first—through every situation and in every calling.

There are no shortcuts. Intimacy is costly. It is not something that can be imparted to you through the simple laying on of hands. You must dig the well of intimacy with your own hands. You must cultivate intimacy before ministry, just as Jesus did. When we live in daily intimate habitation with God, then He can fully activate us to bring true healing and a revelation of son-ship to the world.

ABOUT THE AUTHOR: Sean Feucht is a husband, father, lover, fighter, optimist, musician, speaker, writer, revivalist, and founder of a grassroots global worship, prayer, and missions organization called Burn 24/7. His lifelong quest and dream is to witness a generation of burning hearts arise across the nations of the world with renewed faith, vision, and sacrificial pursuit after the Presence of God with reckless abandon. He has produced, recorded, and released twelve worship albums, numerous teaching resources, and recently coauthored his first book *Fire and Fragrance*. He is married to his gorgeous wife, Kate, and is a new father to their baby girl, Keturah Liv. He currently resides in Harrisburg, Pennsylvania (when he is not on planes, trains, or automobiles). Contact Sean at www.seanfeucht.com and www.burn24-7.com.

EIGHT

�֎

Consecrated Community

By Jeremy Bardwell

The initial wave of Methodist circuit riders spanning across the American frontier had a high value for relationship that is best depicted in their regional weeklong gatherings called the "Camp Meetings." The circuit riders' lives were packed full of itinerate preaching, discipling, marrying and burying, but when it was time to gather for a camp meeting, they would stop everything to fellowship with their comrades and be refreshed in love and commitment for one another.

These meetings would gather people from as far off as fifty miles—a very long wagon ride. There would be times of communion with the Lord, as well as celebratory communion with one another. Many of the riders' lives were so rigorous as they rode to the least and the lost on the American frontier that they were overjoyed just to see that another of their fellow riders lived another year to make it to the meeting.

James B. Finley, a Methodist clergyman and son of an itinerating Methodist pioneer, described the earnest sincerity of the camp meetings in his 1853 autobiography:

> Much may be said about camp meetings, but, take them all in all, for practical exhibition of religion, for unbounded hospitality to strangers, for unfeigned and fervent spirituality, give me a country camp meeting against the world.[5]

The mixture of Holy Ghost manifestations, fiery gospel preaching, and lively fellowship created meetings that no one wanted to miss, including the lost who came to Christ through these meetings. The sacrificial lives of these early circuit riders and their gatherings helped to evangelize the American frontier and establish a Christian foundation in America. It is time to see this same value for relationship and community released again across America and into the nations embodying the same radial devotion and missional spirit modeled by these selfless riders.

God is raising up a new breed of revivalists, though we no longer gallop to remote villages on horseback (unless you're called to Mongolia). However, our core values are consistent with the first wave of Methodist riders. We desire to live true, Biblical community, using the early church as described in the book of Acts as our foundation. Our deep relational commitment to each other will be the key to sustain and fully release the next wave of riders to help fulfill the Great Commission.

What is Community?

At its basic level, the word "community" simply means *common unity*. A community is a group of people who live or work in a specific place, or who share specific interests, goals, and standard of ethics.

As believers, we gather into community for the purpose of worshiping God and seeing revival in our regions. For us, the specific interest is "Just Jesus!" The goal of these communities is "Save the lost, revive the saved, and train and disciple them all." The standard of ethics for these communities is clearly defined through the life and teachings of Jesus Christ. Jesus is our Lord, our Leader, and our Hero. It is the aim of these communities that we would exalt Him above all other pursuits in life, and align ourselves to His Word, will, and ways.

As we continue, let's look at three essentials that must exist within a consecrated community in order for a revival atmosphere to be catalyzed and sustained. These essentials are idol-free living, unity, and an unoffendable heart.

Idol-Free Living:
Nothing Comes Above Adoring and Obeying Jesus

A consecrated community has a foundation of individuals who prioritize and live out what Jesus called the first and greatest commandment: to love the Lord with all your heart, mind, soul, and strength. When these individuals are on fire personally and gather together corporately, their faith, hope, and love compound and the community becomes ablaze as an on-fire, mighty, contending priesthood before God. 1 Peter 2:5 calls us living stones that are being built together into a spiritual house to be a holy priesthood before God.

If our consecrated communities do not carry a strong culture of initiatory love to maintain the first commandment personally, then we will not be the raging inferno God intends as we gather together.

The highest call as a believer will forever be to love the Lord your God with all your heart, with all your soul, with all your mind, and with all your strength (Mark 12:30). This must be the greatest message of a consecrated community. We are set apart for Him and Him alone, both to abide habitually and to obey wholeheartedly—all from the foundation of extravagant love for the most amazing man of all time, Jesus Christ.

The motivation to ride as the early circuit riders, or in our day to do all that God has called us to do, comes from this lifestyle of prioritizing first things first. John Piper, in his book on global missions, *Let the Nations Be Glad*, said that missions exists where worship does not. So you'd better believe that worship is the highest priority where I hang my hat and fellowship with my covenant friends.

The first commandment is not only first and greatest in its impact, it is first and greatest to the heart of God. When this one area is vibrant and healthy in the individuals of a consecrated community, anything is possible. This prospect should stir us to dive deeper into our devotional lives, and from that place, gather our friends to worship together wholeheartedly!

A consecrated community does not exist to remain monastic in its holy pursuit of God alone. The core of that single-minded

existence must lead to individual, regional, and national transformation. One without the other—inward focus without the
outward or vice versa—is not sustainable. Jesus' great commandment and His great commission need to be emphasized and
remain at the core of the culture of a consecrated community.
This culture will create revivalists who live abiding and obeying
instinctually.

The Lord could call that individual into a season of forty
days of prayer and fasting and they would eagerly "come away
with Him." For what food is there on the earth that is better
than the Bread of Life? During that fast, the Lord could call
them into a lifetime of overseas missions to which they would
jump up and down thanking God with emotion in their voice for
the honor to be called to the nations.

You see? To the new breed, there is no separation between
going deep with God and going out with the gospel. They understand that to have long-term gospel impact on society they
must abide in the vine (John 15).

Throughout history, we have seen communities who have
prioritized "separating from society" to seek a deeper interior life
of prayer. We have also seen missional communities that focus
outward on reaching the lost. In this eleventh hour of salvation
history, the next wave of communities will collide these ideals in
a holy marriage to display the fullness of the gospel—love for
Jesus *and* love for the lost. When Jesus and His heart for the lost
is our magnificent obsession, we will see heaven invade earth
through our bold, faith-filled exploits.

Unity

From this place of the first and second commandment working together, the role of Biblical community is to provide an authority, blessing, and a rock-solid perspective that comes through our unity. Unity is essential to vibrant, spiritual life in a community! The scriptural principal of one putting one thousand to flight but two putting ten thousand to flight, shown in Deuteronomy 32:30, is truly powerful in describing the authority that comes from unity among believers.

Matthew 18:19 says,

"Again, I tell you that if two of you on earth agree about anything they ask for, it will be done for them by my Father in heaven."

Unity releases authority. Verse 20 continues,

"For where two or three gather in my name, there am I with them."

Unity also attracts His presence.

Those who live in a consecrated community also know what it means to have to stick to their convictions. However, it is in the place of corporate agreement that our expectations and convictions soar to the next level. Corporate agreement on vision and values creates a worldview through which that community views all of life. The attitude of a consecrated community functioning in unity looks like this:

- No matter the circumstance, revival is a reality.
- The harvest is here, and I am willing to be inconvenienced by the lost.
- The supernatural is natural.

- Nothing is impossible for those who believe.
- Holiness is extremely happy.
- Repentance is wildly joy-filled.
- Prayer is a great and mighty weapon for pulling down strongholds.
- It is my honor to worship God during trying circumstances because He is always worthy.
- I live with my life led by faith first, and my feelings second.

When this attitude and perspective begin to exist in a community with unified agreement, we will see even greater works than Jesus did during His earthly ministry!

Each consecrated community, depending on their commission from the Lord, will have a specific emphasis or mandate that caused the community to develop in the first place. It is very important that there is a deep unity and agreement on that mandate. It is in that unity that God commands a blessing (Psalm 133). There is a night and day difference between living in that blessing and not.

It is through the narrowness of our corporate vision, based on the Word of the Lord, that explosive fruitfulness results. It is also through accomplishing specific, targeted initiatives that our faith is stoked and momentum created. The forward movement of tackling and triumphing over specific tasks within the unified vision is crucial to maintain the electric atmosphere of community life. When we get too broad or vague in our vision, our unity is loosened, our team dynamic is watered down, and our strength is dissipated. From that perspective, it is important that everyone on the team is fully engaged on a heart level with the specific focus of that community. Anything less will cause us to miss the full blessing, authority, and joy that God intends.

The Unoffendable Heart: Sustaining Joy and a Fruitful Impact

As we abide, obey, and walk together in unity, a huge portion of our obedience is not only directed toward the fulfillment of our callings, but also in the standard of conduct in our daily lifestyles. When Jesus is our loving leader, we choose to let even our attitudes be under His command. Living free of offense is the key to sustaining joyful, strong relationships in the midst of pursuing God together.

As a leader of a consecrated community, I can tell you that three of the most deadly sins that crop up in a community are petty offenses, comparison, and jealousy. Jesus faced the temptation of offense when His best friends and His own people betrayed Him. Jesus did much more than simply not steal and never tell a lie. He forgave in His heart without offense when mocked with a purple robe and crown of thorns or as the Jewish crowds cried out to release the notorious prisoner, Barabbas, and sent Jesus away to be crucified. Talk about an opportunity for offense. When we begin to meditate on the magnificence of Jesus and what He was like, it makes us want to be more like Him... unoffendable.

Consider Philippians 2:1-8 (NKJV):

> Therefore if there is any consolation in Christ, if any comfort of love, if any fellowship of the Spirit, if any affection and mercy, fulfill my joy by being like-minded, having the same love, being of one accord,

of one mind. Let nothing be done through selfish ambition or conceit, but in lowliness of mind let each esteem others better than himself. Let each of you look out not only for his own interests, but also for the interests of others. Let this mind be in you which was also in Christ Jesus, who being in the form of God, did not consider it robbery to be equal with God, but made himself of no reputation, taking the form of a bondservant, and coming in the likeness of men. And being found in the appearance as a man, he humbled himself and became obedient to the point of death, even the death of the cross.

Our petty relational conflicts are not even worthy of comparing to what Jesus went through, and yet He remained without offense. When we realize what Jesus has done for us, it brings heaven's perspective into our current circumstance. Comparison, jealousy, and offense have to go when we begin to understand the cross and Christ's deep love for us. When a community is made up of individuals who are secure in Jesus's love and whose life-long pursuit is to imitate Christ, then their interpersonal relationships come into a wonderful, healthy, and offense-free place.

Imagine a community free of gossip, slander, and backbiting. Imagine a community that walks out Biblical confrontation and truly fights for the highest calling on each other's lives. Imagine a community where promotions and achievements are celebrated instead of causing resentment and comparison. This is how we were meant to live and to achieve our high callings in God.

A Community that Releases Strength and Perspective

When the three elements of idol-free living, unity, and an unoffendable heart are in place in a community, the result serves the practical needs of providing strength, rest, training, discipleship, and fresh faith to revival-minded individuals. The original circuit riders knew that every good rider needed a place to park his horse. In fact, The First Discipline of the Methodist church stated, "Be merciful to your Beast. Not only ride moderately, but see with your own Eyes that your Horse is rubbed and fed."[6] They saw value in a specific place to rest and regain strength even for their horses.

The first wave of circuit-rider heroes was wildly radical in their pursuit to see the least and the lost saved by Jesus Christ. Many of the early Methodist riders died before the age of thirty-three because of exposure to the elements and diseases as they rode to the remote towns on the American frontier. I believe that with the same passion harnessed in Biblical wisdom, the next wave of riders in this generation can live long lives, raise healthy children, have strong marriages, and leave twice the impact through their simple obedience. There is nothing holy about dying young, but it is indeed a clear indicator of the level of commitment to the cause.

I believe God is highlighting community so that commitment, sustainability, and fruitfulness can increase. We must be wise in these days to live every aspect of our lives from a scriptural foundation in order to unlock the full potential God has for all of us.

As we look to our foundation in the book of Acts, we see that they had an utmost value for community. Not only was it in the place of community that the Holy Spirit dropped on Pentecost, it was also how the fire of the Spirit was sustained.

> And they continued steadfastly in the apostles' doctrine and fellowship, in the breaking of bread, and in prayers. Then fear came upon every soul and many wonders and signs were done through the apostles. Now all who believed were together, and had all things in common, and sold their possessions and goods and divided them among all, as anyone had need. So continuing daily with one accord in the temple, and breaking bread from house to house, they ate their food with gladness and simplicity of heart, praising God and having favor with all the people, and the Lord added to the church daily those who were being saved. —Acts 2:42-47 (NKJV)

It's so wonderful to see that the simple things that make up the most basic community—fellowship and the breaking of bread—were integral to lives being changed, signs and wonders, and the release of the fear of the Lord. Community was a great source of strength and power as they saw incredible advances for the kingdom of God.

Some may say that true book-of-Acts community is out of reach for us today. I would argue that without a book-of-Acts community, our dreams and the dreams of God are out of our reach. Their unity was intentional and purposeful, their generosity was willing and joyful, and their power undeniable as their anointing grew out of their love for Jesus and for each other. I believe that as we reorient our lives in the same way the apostles did, we will see similar results manifest in our cities and regions.

There was consecrated community when the Holy Spirit poured Himself out on the day of Pentecost. Consecrated community later sustained Peter and John when they were arrested and brought before the Sanhedrin. That same community responded in prayer that changed natural events (Acts 4). Once surrounded in that atmosphere of faith, they were able to properly process the persecution, turn it around into fuel for their prayers, and see great boldness manifested among the believers. What the enemy meant as intimidation, led to a prayer meeting that supernaturally shook a building and released passionate men and women into the countryside who turned the region upside down.

> And being let go, **they went to their own companions** and reported all that the chief priests and elders had said to them. So when they heard that, they raised their voice to God with one accord and said: "Lord, You are God, who made heaven and earth and the sea, and all that is in them, who by the mouth of Your servant David have said:
>
> 'Why did the nations rage, and the people plot vain things? The kings of the earth took their stand, and the rulers were gathered together against the Lord and against His Christ.'
>
> For truly against Your holy Servant Jesus, whom You anointed, both Herod and Pontius Pilate, with the Gentiles and the people of Israel, were gathered

together to do whatever Your hand and Your purpose determined before to be done. Now, Lord, look on their threats, and grant to Your servants that **with all boldness** they may speak Your word, by stretching out Your hand to heal, and that signs and wonders may be done through the name of Your holy Servant Jesus."

And when they had prayed, **the place where they were assembled** together was shaken; and they were all filled with the Holy Spirit, and they **spoke the word of God with boldness.** —Acts 4:23-31 (NKJV)

Community is for the purpose of sustaining world-changing boldness in the face of great opposition. Imagine communities shaking and changing under the power of God, birthing movements of faith and boldness. Imagine one of these communities being planted at each college campus in America. This is a recipe for a light and darkness showdown, and we know which always wins. Revival is a reality. The harvest is now.

The Day and the Hour for Community and Team

Everyone lives in some kind of community, even if that community is your family, colleagues at work, you and your roommate, or your neighbors next door. No matter what kind of community you find yourself in right now, you can promote the values of a consecrated community and do your part to make your community a place where the kingdom of God can come and be established.

Creating and sustaining a culture of revival in community means that we choose to follow Jesus with all that is within us;

we live in unity and wholeheartedly engage in the focus of our community; we maintain an unoffended heart through forgiveness, avoiding comparison and jealousy; and we release strength and perspective to those around us so that we can run and win the race that God has set before each of us.

The need for consecrated community centered on the presence of God is going to increase as we approach the end of the age. The wheat and the tares will grow side by side until the return of Jesus (Matthew 13:24). The darkest days are ahead for the world, yet the greatest, brightest days remain for the body of Christ. This darkness will be marked by deception and unbelief; the Scripture says that even some of the elect will go astray (Matthew 13:22). This is not meant to produce fear, for the battle is already won. However, gathering in intentional community and enthroning Him with your praise will bring an authority and corporate perspective that will sustain a thriving impact on the earth until Jesus' feet touch the ground.

God is raising many beacons of light and truth that together will punch a hole in the heavens, bind the strongmen, and lead to a massive plundering of his goods. This can only happen if we gather and enthrone Him.

When Jesus taught us to pray for His kingdom to come and His will to be done on earth as it is in heaven, He was teaching us to ask for more than just an invasion of the miraculous. He was praying that the very throne of God would be established on the earth in willing, often musical, love from every tribe, tongue and nation. He was teaching us to pray that the atmosphere that surrounds His throne in heaven would invade earth. After all, it is in this atmosphere that no sickness, death, demon, or sin can survive. These communities will be open heavens, releasing all the light and power of heaven onto the earth.

The circuit riders are rising again. These riders will reap a harvest like never before in the history of America. We must prepare like Noah for the very thing we see coming, ready the communities for training, and set this army free to soar. Where are the community builders who will create the practical structure to house and train thousands? Where are the squad leaders who will mobilize bands of riders from the place of consecrated community unto commissioning for nations?

The time is now for the community leaders to arise who will touch many nations by gathering, discipling, and launching hundreds of thousands into their callings. Will you respond by breaking out of your insecurity and rise to the needs present in our generation? It is time. It is what our generation is crying out for, and it is what we have the answer for. Let us decide now to throw ourselves completely into what God is doing on the earth. Let the consecrated communities arise.

ABOUT THE AUTHOR: Jeremy Bardwell is the husband of Natalie and a father of three beautiful children. He is one of the pioneers with a team of covenant friends of Fire and Fragrance whose dream is to see "consecrated communities, centered around the presence of God, leading to revival and reformation, planted in every nation of the earth." Jeremy is currently leading a growing Fire and Fragrance community in Harrisburg, Pennsylvania, with a vision to see revival on the Ivy League Universities. Jeremy's passion is to see young leaders discipled and raised up with a vision for worldwide revival and reformation. Follow Jeremy Bardwell at twitter.com/jeremybardwell, facebook.com/jerbardwell, and www.bardwellblog.com.

❖

NINE

Grounded in the Word

By Taylor Stutts

I grew up with a fair bit of knowledge about the Bible. I went to church, Sunday school, and Vacation Bible Schools in the summer. I also attended a private Christian school where I was taught the Bible, had memory verse assignments, and special weeks devoted to spiritual life.

However, during most of that time I struggled with my relationship with God. I wondered if He was really there. I wondered if what I had been taught was true. I wondered if I would be a Christian had I been born in another country. Is this my lot in life? What is my purpose for being here? I had many questions and went through highs and lows regarding my beliefs. The Christians I knew did not inspire me. The church did not seem exciting or dynamic.

My views changed when two of my older brother's friends came back from a place called YWAM (Youth With a Mission). These men had a new focus in life. No longer were they intent on simply following the crowd. God was no longer a fairy tale story. They told me amazing miracle stories of God and how He had become real to them. I felt I had to go and find out for myself.

During my senior year of high school, I started thinking about college. I'd heard exhilarating stories of parties, girls, and football games on campuses with thousands of people. Despite all that, I couldn't get away from this tug on my heart, "What if God is real?" I could risk gaining nothing and losing everything. I was craving for something real—something I could live or die for. When the time came, I decided to go to YWAM.

I headed to YWAM Maui for a six-month Discipleship Training School (DTS). It was my last effort to find God and it was going to be God's last chance to prove He was real. I was either going to be sold out for Christ once and for all, or I was going to go to college and do whatever I desired. The very first day of DTS, God met me in an amazing and personal way during a lecture called "Hearing God's Voice." In one moment, my entire life was changed forever—simply because of one true encounter with the living God.

He was everything I had heard and dreamed about and more. I wanted all that God had to offer. I became hungry to know God intimately and passionately, and I felt everyone else needed to know this truth. The Bible also changed. It was no longer just a homework assignment, part of my to-do list, or something to make me feel less guilty about my life. When I read the Bible, I discovered God in ways I never knew existed, and I began to see His Word confirm everything I had experienced.

The Bible became a great gateway to the knowledge of God. It satisfied my life more than anything else I could imagine. It pierced my heart and my mind every time I read it. I was so in love with God and His Word, I would often fall asleep with the Bible on my chest, laid open to a new favorite passage I had read.

I still had many questions, but I had a deeper hunger for God. My questions and my hunger began working together in a dynamic way, and I began to grow in my relationship with Him. I learned that the Bible had the answer to any of my questions. I just needed God's help to open my eyes to see it and give me revelation.

Up until I began to study the Word at YWAM, I never felt very smart. I didn't think I could come to understand the Bible, but Jesus changed everything. My hunger drove me to learn all that I could. I discovered that the Bible was a well of living water.

The Authority of Scripture

I learned the history of the Bible and became convinced that this book was different from all others on the planet. The Bible was written over a period of fifteen hundred years, by forty authors, on three continents, in three languages. Yet, it contains a consistent message that accurately describes life. It comprehensively describes the condition of the human heart and soul.

The Bible gives us the right understanding of where we came from, whom God is, how we are to live, our purpose in life, and where we all are going. It is the source of all truth. Truth, however, is not just a concept; truth is found in Jesus Christ. Jesus Himself said,

> "I am the way, the truth, and the life. No one comes to the Father except through me." —John 14:6 (NKJV)

We must rely on the Word of God to guide us if we are going to impact our culture and world. As revivalists, if we have a right understanding of the Bible, God's Word will go deep into our hearts. Then we will not only experience revival, but also reformation as we live out the revelation.

The Bible is our supreme authority. There is no higher power to appeal to. The source of the Bible is God, who has all authority. God cannot lie (Hebrews 6:18) so we can trust His Word to be true. God's Word leads our lives and societies into radical transformation and glory. Anything else governing our lives leads to spiritual bankruptcy and destruction. He shows us in His Word the pattern for our lives. He has given us the foundation to the kingdom of God, and the strategy to build it.

When we align our lives in accordance with His Word, then we are living in revival authority. When we know the authority of His Word and preach it, it has power to transform any life.

> Then Jesus said to those Jews who believed Him, "If you abide in My Word, you are my disciples indeed. And you shall know the truth, and the truth will set you free." —John 8:31-32 (NKJV)

If we want to call ourselves disciples of Jesus, we must abide in His Word. If we want to be set free and if we want to set others free, we must know the truth—we must abide in His Word. There is nothing more joyful than freedom in Christ. God's truth will break the lies in our life, and we will discover the abundant life that Christ provides. There is no higher authority than what God has given us in His Word. As we preach His promises, others are able to believe those promises. God will always honor His Word.

When a community lives under the authority of the Word, it is no longer ruled by its feelings and emotions. When we let the Scripture dictate our lives, we allow our feelings to follow. We are no longer following the thoughts or feelings of another person. We are agreeing with and obeying God's Word. Living according to God's Word shatters the fear of man. We no longer have to worry about what others think. When we are living and doing what God says, we can live satisfied knowing we are pleasing God.

The Spirit and The Truth

When we add the anointing of the Holy Spirit to the Word, it is like mixing nitrogen and glycerin. Some of the greatest changes in history can be traced back to a faithful follower of Christ declaring God's Word.

Dwight L. Moody was born in Massachusetts in 1837. His family was poor and his father passed away when he was four years old. Moody attended four years of school, and at the age of ten he went to work to support his family. The odds were certainly against Moody ever succeeding in the eyes of the world. Everything changed, however, when he gave his heart and life to Jesus at eighteen. He became hungry for God, and his source of education was the Word of God. He moved to the worst part of Chicago and started a Sunday school for orphaned children.

Moody, a man who grew up without a father, was used by God to become a father figure for many. He taught the children the love of the heavenly Father.

Moody never let his circumstances hold him back. His credentials came from God's Word and his unwavering trust in those words and promises. In fact, Moody loved the Word of God so much that he started a highly respected Bible college in Chicago called the Moody Bible Institute. The Institute is still training people in the Word of God today. He traveled over one million miles, preached to more than one hundred million people, and personally led an estimated 750,000 people to Christ.

Through the power of the Holy Spirit, Moody went on to become the greatest evangelist of his time. He helped lead America and England into a glorious period of revival. He carried the understanding of walking in the power of the Spirit and the authority of the Word.

Like Moody, most of Jesus' disciples were not considered exceptionally educated men before they spent time with the Lord. In the book of Acts, we see that they preached a simple gospel and it transformed the world. In Acts 4:13 we read,

> When they saw the courage of Peter and John and realized that they were unschooled, ordinary men, they were astonished and they took note that these men had been with Jesus.

What a testimony! And this can be the testimony of today's generation of revivalists. If we love and follow Jesus, He promises to guide us into the ultimate truth.

"And I will pray to the Father, and He will give you another Helper, that He may abide with you forever—the Spirit of truth, whom the world cannot receive, because it neither sees Him nor knows Him; but you know Him, for He dwells with you and will be in you." —John 14:16-17 (NKJV)

From Revival to Reformation

After I fully surrendered my life to God, I had much zeal to do great things for Him. The problem was that most of my life to that point had been built on what others thought, my own fears, and my insecurities—not on God. I had a lot of passion but not much character that reflected God's character. I needed some serious discipleship. My passion needed to be directed by God's Word.

It is not good to have zeal without knowledge, nor to be hasty and miss the way. —Proverbs 19:2

God's Word became the standard of my life to match the zeal in my heart. Knowing Christ's character and acting like Him is "the way" Proverbs says we cannot miss. Learning and becoming takes time and testing. There is no fast track to Godly character.

The Word guided my zeal in the right direction so that I could walk and be fruitful in "the way." Revolutionaries must sustain their character and anointing to bear long-term fruit. God will increase authority on the hearts of the humble to display His power. The passionate heart of a revolutionary must be refined and reformed by God's Word. It cannot be shaped by anything else.

The Bible gives a remarkable account of how the Word of God brings revival and reformation. In 2 Chronicles 34-35, we read of Josiah, the boy who became king at the age of eight. He came from a long line of rebellious and wicked people. Both his father and grandfather led the nation of Israel to do evil in sight of God.

Needless to say, there were not many godly examples for him to follow. But there was something different about Josiah. When he was sixteen years old, he broke the pattern of rebellion towards God and "began to seek the God of his father David" (2 Chronicles 34:3). Four years later, he started an awakening in his nation by destroying all the idols and worship of false gods.

> He tore down the altars and the Asherah poles, crushed the idols to powder, and cut to pieces all the incense altars throughout Israel. —2 Chronicles 34:7

When Josiah was twenty-six, the book of the law was discovered in the temple. Most people believe that it was the book of Deuteronomy. As the scroll was read aloud to the king, he was overcome with emotion and tore his clothes. Josiah was already living in personal revival, but when he heard the Word of God he discovered there was more.

From a young age, Josiah had been filled with passion and zeal for God. I believe he was living in obedience to all that he knew until this point. Then he discovered that there was an even greater standard. He discovered new principles and laws to build his nation. Through this he was able to reform his nation, bringing them into alignment with God's Word.

He restored true worship in his country and put God's Word in its rightful place. He invoked the nation to celebrate one of the most important feasts in the Old Testament—the Passover.

> The Passover had not been observed like this in Israel since the days of the prophet Samuel; and none of the kings of Israel had ever celebrated such a Passover as did Josiah, with the priests, the Levites, and all Judah and Israel who were there with the people of Jerusalem. —2 Chronicles 35:18

God's Word moved his passion and zeal in the right direction. It became the focal point of his life and it governed how he led. He took his nation from a place of revival to reformation. It is one thing to get excited about something for a little while. It is another thing when excitement turns into a lifelong commitment, shaping everything about us. God's Word still carries the power to pierce any heart and bring people to repentance.

God can do today what He did in the time of Josiah. God will soften the hearts of kings and presidents, and enable them to receive Him. God's Word brought revival to Israel, tearing down false worship and raising up true worship. The Word gave them the instructions that reformed their society. When they followed God, it brought them into joy, feasting, and celebration.

Governments and political systems are failing all over the world. If we build upon the foundations in the Bible, we will not crumble. God's kingdom is everlasting and there will be no end to the increase of His government. The nations are longing for truth that will bring them into joy everlasting. We must not mock or stand back when nations are struggling. We must be ready to serve and bring in the gospel truths that will lift a nation up. If we are not ready, nations will accept a new system that will most likely end up worse than the one before.

In the nineteenth century, one man was disturbed by the economic and social conditions in Europe. This man was an atheist; therefore, he didn't believe that God or the Bible would provide any solutions to the problems he saw. He went on to write one of the most influential books in history, *The Communist Manifesto*. This man was Karl Marx.

Marx saw the greed of the rich and devastation to the poor. He created a system that he thought would solve this problem and presented a utopian society. However, the foundation of his solution had no room for God and assumed every person is inherently good. The god in this system was the economic wellbeing of each person.

Marx's ideas circulated and fell into the hands of violent revolutionaries. These men overthrew governments and instilled their belief system in society. Anyone who stood against their ideals was eliminated. Many people who could not produce in society were slaughtered because they were an economic burden. Human life had no value; money, power, and production were prized above all else. Millions were put to death in nations like the former Soviet Union, China, and Cambodia.

Some of these principles still influence many countries, including the United States. We have lost sight of the value of human life. We have opened the door to euthanasia and abortion. We are taught to believe these practices enhance our society when in fact they are destroying the very heart of our culture.

This is why we must proclaim the truth contained in the Word of God. It has been said that all that is necessary for the triumph of evil is that good men do nothing. However, according to Jesus, everything is possible to those who believe (Mark 9:23).

A Culture of the Word

Let's have the Bible become precious to us today. Let gratefulness fill our hearts for the scribes and monks who faithfully and meticulously transcribed the books of the Bible, one letter at a time. We must honor former revivalists who were killed for translating the Bible into common languages for everyone to read and understand.

If we do not cherish what we have and use it to bring breakthroughs for our world today, we are forfeiting part of the inheritance for which our forefathers died. They are standing in the great cloud of witnesses waiting for us to pick up where they left off.

If we hold fast to the truths of the Bible, we won't be easily led astray by the lies of this world. With God's truth in our hearts, we will be able to see greed, envy, idol worship, sexual impurity, hatred, and all the other sins of this world in their true light. We will be aware of the schemes of the enemy to break down righteousness in our culture, and we will understand how the devil wants to desensitize our generation to God's holiness and purity.

God wants us to be counter-culture revolutionaries who live our lives to please God and not man. It takes brave men and women to pursue revival and reformation. We need to first live out the truths of the Scriptures so we can have authority in what we preach. Our testimony will give others the freedom to follow in our footsteps. If we can stand firm on God's Word with love and kindness, we can present real solutions to the problems in our society.

It may not be pretty—people will hate us, persecute us, and falsely accuse us, but in the end we will be rewarded. We will see a changed culture and a liberated people. More importantly, our Father in heaven will be proud, for we will be standing upon His Word for the sake of righteousness.

As revivalists, we must spend time in the Word of God daily. It is the book of life and life abundant. It is the manual for all of life. We must want His Word to be written on our hearts and our lips so we can speak the truth. How can we say we know Jesus unless we are searching what is written about Him and living life with Him?

When we align ourselves with the Word, we are aligning ourselves with God and we are able to receive the promises and power of the kingdom. The more we know the Word of God, the more pure and precise our prophetic insight and revelation will become. His Word will give us strength to overcome. When we see a generation fall in love with God's Word, our culture will change.

There are so many benefits to knowing the Word of God. I've mentioned many in this chapter. Also consider that when we know and are living His Word, we will...

- See God's original design and the areas of our culture that are out of alignment.

- Have revival authority from the Word in our hearts to tear down strongholds.
- Have fire in our hearts.
- Support a culture of life.
- Understand how to impact the world around us.
- Grow in our knowledge and love for God.
- Understand His heart, and be His heart to those around us.
- Bind up the brokenhearted and set the captives free.
- Have good news for everyone.
- Lead from a place of revival to reformation.
- Disciple nations.
- Have faith for the impossible.
- Bring heaven to earth.

When the Word of God governs our lives and our culture, it will be impossible for revival not to break out. Psalm 16:11 declares:

> You have made known to me the path of life; You will fill me with joy in your presence, with eternal pleasures at your right hand.

With the Word of God as our foundation, God will make known His path of life to us. The result is joy and eternal pleasures in His presence. I want that! Do you?

Prayer for the Word

Pray this out loud with me right now:

Father, I repent of apathy and passivity in reading Your Word. I repent for a lack of zeal over Your truth. Tear down the stronghold of lies I have believed. Remove the lying emotion of boredom. Break off any lie of difficulty or the lie that I won't understand. I ask You for a spirit of wisdom and revelation to fill me. Come Holy Spirit, teach me and guide me in Your truth. Give me a hunger for the Word. I set my heart to know the depths of the knowledge of God. Eliminate compromise in my life. I joyfully align myself to Your Word. I will instantly obey what You teach me. Give me the strength to stand for truth in every circumstance. Put the fire of Your Word deep in my heart, and let the fire of Your Word spill out of my lips to a generation. Open my eyes to see all that You want me to see. I want to fall more in love with You.

ABOUT THE AUTHOR: Taylor Stutts and his wife, Julia, are a part of the Fire and Fragrance community based out of Kona, Hawaii, and Taylor brings leadership over the training schools. They long to see a generation fall in love with the presence of God and have a passion to see revival and reformation in the nations. Contact Taylor at www.ywamstutts.com.

TEN

❖

No Eye Has Seen

By Sean Feucht

In my thirtieth year, in the fourth month on the fifth day,
while I was among the exiles by the Kebar River, the
heavens were opened and I saw visions of God.
—Ezekiel 1:1

G od ordains our days "before one of them came to be" (Psalm 139:16). He initiates strategic and divine God-encounters that serve as markers, ignition points, and signposts in our lives that keep us on track and hook us deeper into His unfolding plan. Throughout history, the greatest revival leaders of the kingdom have been marked by such encounters. God loves to pull out these surprises at the most unlikely places and times. His surprises carry the ultimate shock value.

These encounters are moments when His destiny confronts our apathy and we receive an invitation to align our lives with heaven. Every person longs to claim authentic interaction with something bigger and greater than themselves. Even the most successful, rich, and powerful people ache for supernatural intervention in their lives. This longing is inherent in every human heart above all other longings and is frequently amplified by the cultural icons of the day. As the actress Juliette Binoche remarked, "My ambition in life is to have beautiful encounters, not to make money."

The prophet Ezekiel's purpose for living unfolded through a series of encounters, trances, and visions. He was commissioned to "eat the scroll" of destiny (Ezekiel 3:1) and then "go to the house of Israel and speak my words" (Ezekiel 3:4). Called to boldly deliver some of the harshest and most intense "sermons" contained in the Bible, Ezekiel must have consistently returned to those initial encounters to sustain, uphold, and guide him through his life mandate. Plagued by misunderstanding, ill treatment, and scorn from his own people, Ezekiel's journey reveals the strong deterrents we can face when we encounter God and boldly step into our destiny.

In the same way, the greatest men and women in the Bible were confronted, perplexed, inspired, and commissioned from these signposts of significance. Abraham was beckoned to count the stars. Moses beheld the burning bush. Gideon was scared stiff and was then prophesied to by an angel. Balaam's donkey suddenly knew his language. An angel told Mary that she'd conceive the Messiah not by a man, but by the Holy Spirit. Paul was knocked off his horse by a light from heaven. And the revelator John went into an open-heaven vision concerning the last days. There are too many stories to list. God has His own ways of getting our attention. He certainly knew how to get mine.

Downgrade is the New Upgrade

I will never forget when we loaded up the car that frigid Oklahoma morning in January 2007. Within twenty-four hours from receiving a direct word from the Lord, my wife and I were downsizing from our spacious, beautiful, new home to a well-worn, four-door 1998 Toyota Camry. Most would call that a significant downgrade. We felt only excitement and nervous tension coursing through our veins that frosty morning. It felt like the crispness of the air was charged with opportunity and pregnant with possibility.

We had no idea where we were going or what we were doing. We were surrendered to being guided solely by our encounter. It was the only option. One very powerful principle comes to my heart as I recount this story: the way down is always the way up in the kingdom.

Fueled by the prayers and prophetic words spoken over us on our wedding day one year earlier, our wholehearted agreement resounded to the words, "releasing fire to the nations around the world." This is why my wife and I were as surprised as anyone when our first year appeared completely contradictory to that word. Instead, we entered into a season of unexpected comfort, ease, and stability. We also never left home. There was no risk, crazy adventure, or foreign soil under our feet in that first year.

We were almost completely stationary and never left our town (much less neighborhood) of Tulsa, Oklahoma.

I grew up in a missionary home where my family traveled from Kathmandu, Nepal, to Ghana, West Africa, to Iquitos, Peru, all before springtime in any given year. So it felt like cultural whiplash to be so motionless. Everything was too still. Yet there was something I embraced in the stability, serenity, and consistency of it all. It seemed as if everything I stood against was now my situated reality—the safe and suburban American dream. What startled me even more was how good it felt to be in that place. For once in my twenty-two years, I enjoyed settling into a seemingly normal life. I was finally able to enjoy the greener pasture that lay on the other side…or so I thought.

That first year God had blessed us with two amazing jobs that provided for all of our needs, an incredible community of authentic friendships, and a burgeoning underground gathering of lovesick worshippers and musicians. I dub it "underground" because we did not have any titles, structures, or even a cool ministry name. In stark contrast to the Bible-Belt landscape of well-known mega-churches and long-standing Christian television ministries, what was now emerging in the passion and rawness of night and day worship was anything but polished and traditional. There was something fresh about it.

Just like the men on the road to Emmaus, our hearts were burning every time we gathered together to host His presence in worship. That simple saying caught wind and (at the risk of sounding like an arsonist cult) we began to call our humble gatherings "Burn." There was a wildness and undignified nature about the worship, prayer, and community that was gathering together to host these presence-led extended hours of worship and prayer.

Many times we would accidentally stay up worshipping all through the night. Gifted musicians were transforming before our very eyes—from jaded cynics to child-like enthusiasts. Pastors were breaking out of their self-imposed religious boxes into incredible freedom. The "Burn" became a watering hole for the thirsty in the city to come and drink deep. We were more than thrilled to simply be a fly on the wall and watch all that God was doing.

3 a.m. Tsunami Crash

I was pretty content and secure at this point in my life. I could put check marks on my inventory dream list: beautiful wife, college degree, amazing job, perfect house and cars (I even had a convertible), thriving ministry, and authentic friendships. But it was not enough. God wanted more of me. He wanted ALL. And deep down in the core of my being, I wanted more too.

The signpost of significance in my life came through waves upon waves of dreams, visions, and even audible voices crashing onto the shores of my tidy and domesticated life. The Holy Spirit or "Holy Harasser" was relentless in hunting down God's destiny over my life and often interrupted me at the most inconvenient moments. The final tsunami crash came as the Psalm 132 Davidic mantra was once again emblazoned into my heart in middle of the night during a dream (for the tenth time). This was the final wave. I could not escape and it pushed me over the edge.

> He swore an oath to the LORD, he made a vow to the Mighty One of Jacob: "I will not enter my house

or go to my bed, I will allow no sleep to my eyes
or slumber to my eyelids, till I find a place for the
LORD, a dwelling for the Mighty One of Jacob."
                                        —Psalm 132:2–5

This was the cry of David's heart that rang like a clarion
trumpet blast throughout his entire life. Birthed in the secret
places of the Judean hills while tending sheep, then cultivated
for ten years while hanging on to God's promise to be king (or
running for his life from Saul), this same cry manifested loud
and clear when he finally assumed the throne. David wanted to
establish a resting place for God's presence 24/7/365. He would
not stop until that dream became a reality: day and night worship and adoration that never ends.

At 3 a.m. the same mantra of King David became the language expressing the longing of my heart. Just as a great spiritual
father and friend, Lou Engle, once wrote to me:

> The leaders that move history give articulation to that
> which is already silently rumbling in the collective
> conscience of the masses. When that articulated word
> is released, bones rattle and great people movements
> begin to shake the earth.

My bones began to rattle and a movement inside me was
activated. This moment clearly became my "no turning back"
commissioning from above. It did not come at a packed out con-
ference or a hyped-up event. There were not a slew of famous
apostles and prophets laying their hands to confirm God's calling. It was in the darkness, stillness, and somewhat loneliness
of the 3 a.m. wakeup call that God landed a holy defibrillator

to my chest. After months of resisting, it only took a matter of mere seconds and my heart was finally penetrated, captivated, and recalibrated.

I love the quote from George Eliot, which says, "It is never too late to be what you might have been." In the encounter of that moment, my inner groans reverberated and my soul could no longer be silenced. I could no longer buy and keep my stock in the predictability of the American Dream though admittedly I had begun to enjoy it. I knew it was too safe, pretty, and contained for what I was made for. It was time to un-domesticate my domesticated heart. I was called to build resting places of His presence all over the world. I did not know how or where. But after this encounter, I knew why.

Sometimes the "why" is the most crucial element to understanding. I knew Jesus came to earth and died for more than the life I was living. Risking it all was the only way out...or the only way deeper in.

From Existence to Significance

I will never forget the day my heart began to explode with expectation at the glorious unknown ahead. A nervous and giddy tension was welling up inside my wife and me. We had absolutely no idea where God was leading us or what our lives would look like in the future. We had little money and no jobs or house. We simply drove away on a promise and prophetic word. It all seemed so risky, unconventional, and even foolish to some (and many loudly shared those opinions).

After all the years of preparation through schools, college degrees, and the beginnings of a successful entrepreneurship, it now seemed like a waste. Were we really supposed to simply throw all that hard work away and follow some fantasy? Aren't there verses in the book of Proverbs speaking directly against such foolish notions? These were some of the thoughts that bombarded the already clogged traffic of my brain that day.

But all I knew is that my heart was coming alive. Isn't this the gospel of the kingdom that Jesus taught, lived, and died for? Is not the call to lose our lives to gain it all? Didn't He condemn the Pharisees whose minds were puffed up with pride, but their hearts were like whitewashed tombs? It was time for me to stop living only out of the knowledge in my head and start living from the burning of my heart.

I desperately wanted my life to move from merely existing as a Christian voice in this world to becoming a significant echo in halls of eternity. I kept thinking of the good jobs and stable lives that Peter, John, and Matthew likely had before Jesus crashed in on them that day with the simple call to "follow Me." They did not hesitate or even count the cost, but "straightaway left their nets, and followed him" (Matthew 4:19-20).

My heart longed to humbly follow in these dangerously ordinary pioneers' footsteps. The narrow road of risk was the only option and faith was the currency to pay the way. Jesus was clear that the only way to save your life so that it would be significant in heaven is to lose it here in our temporary life on earth.

I was ready to lose everything to gain everything.

> "For whoever desires to save his life will lose it, but whoever loses his life for my sake will save it. For

what profit is it to a man if he gains the whole world,
and is himself destroyed or lost?"

—Luke 9:24-25 (NKJV)

It seemed like my entire life was somewhat predictable up until this point. I went to a Christian high school, Spirit-filled liberal arts university, kept up a 4.0 GPA, and obtained my degree. I then started a real estate business, got married to the girl of my dreams, and began living life. I had grown up in a stable home with parents that were more than good Christians—they were my personal heroes of ultimate sacrifice for the sake of Christ. They gave up their careers, money, and notoriety to spill out love across the world—spreading the healing of Jesus to the most unreached nations on the planet.

I should have known that this generational legacy and heritage would soon hunt me down. It seems the writing was already clearly written on the wall for my life.

No Eye Has Seen

As I now stand back and view all God has accomplished and released since that cold winter morning in January 2007, I am utterly astounded. I would never have dreamed that so much would be possible in a single lifetime—let alone just five short years of complete dependency. I have now tasted and seen of His goodness, provision, and miracles, and do not want to live any other way.

We have been privileged to witness cities and nations set ablaze with uncontrollable wildfires of worship and prayer. Books and training manuals have been written, and fiery albums carrying the sound of prophetic worship have been captured and released. Training schools have been raised up and are sending out a steady stream of revivalists and "musician-aries" to the darkest places on earth. The tent pegs of the tabernacle of David (Amos 9:11) are now being firmly secured in the soil of nations, and communities are raising the banner of intimacy and sonship. Revelation of kingdom and revival culture is invading and replacing the false ideologies of complacency, greed, and an egocentric gospel. Widespread salvation, healings, and extravagant breakthroughs are abounding as joy-filled lovers of God are willing to lose their lives, even unto death.

God is moving and there is no better time to be alive. We are not ashamed to shout from the rooftops all God has done because our boast is not in ourselves but in the Lord. The words of Paul to the early church echo through the testimonies, stories, and teachings you have just read.

> For even if I should boast somewhat more about our authority, which the Lord gave us for edification, and not for your destruction. I shall not be ashamed.
> —2 Corinthians 10:8 (NKJV)

You, the reader, have just been blasted by a fire hydrant of edification that carries massive authority. These are not merely good ideas; they are foundational arrows of truth for an emerging kingdom culture. I pray this pierces the depths of your heart and leaves you ruined for a normal life. The Holy Spirit inside keeps yelling to me that we have not seen anything yet.

The kingdom is always advancing, increasing, and expanding all over the world at a rate none of us can fathom. For the in-

crease of His government over nations, systems, and cultures—
there shall be no end (Isaiah 9:7). This is only the beginning.
There is more…there is always much more.

Just as with the parable of the workers in Matthew 20, we
are the eleventh hour workers positioned to step into a breakthrough—a divine moment that we did not pay the price for.
How humbling and sobering this is to our hearts and how
damaging to our pride. We are truly standing on the shoulders
of giants.

Isaiah cried out to the Lord,

> Oh, that you would rend the heavens and come
> down, that the mountains would tremble before you!
> As when fire sets twigs ablaze and causes water to
> boil, come down to make your name known to your
> enemies and cause the nations to quake before you!
> For when you did awesome things that we did not
> expect, you came down, and the mountains trembled
> before you. Since ancient times no one has heard, no
> ear has perceived, no eye has seen any God besides
> you, who acts on behalf of those who wait for him.
>
> —Isaiah 64:1-4

I, too, cry out, "Rend the heavens, oh God, and come down!
Come and make Your name known in the earth!" Will you join
that cry?

No ear has heard nor eye has seen any god except our God
who acts on behalf of those who pursue His presence and wait
for Him. Are we ready to dive into the ocean of God's discovery

for all this verse holds for our lives? Do we long to move from mere existence on this temporal earth to significance in eternity? We were made for so much more.

Today is the day and this is the time. Is your heart pounding yet? Is that nervous, giddy, and expectant feeling coursing like electricity through your veins? This moment could be your own signpost of significance. This could be not just the ending of a chapter, but the beginning of a new book for the rest of your life.

The outpouring is upon us and is already here. His presence has begun to rain down on the nations of the world. What would happen if a generation of leaders—postured from the place of humility, intimacy, and sacrifice—embraced the values of kingdom culture? What if they threw themselves into the middle of God's outpouring already taking place around the world? I believe these days are those once prophesied by Daniel, Joel, the disciples, and Jesus.

Responding to the bewildered crowd witnessing the outpouring of fire Jesus promised, Peter declared, "…this is what was spoken by the prophet Joel" (Acts 2:16). We are also in such a day where *this* which is happening is *that* which has been spoken of.

> "And afterward,
> I will pour out my Spirit on all people.
> Your sons and daughters will prophesy,
> your old men will dream dreams,
> your young men will see visions." —Joel 2:28

In concluding this book, we desire to call you to a full-scale adoption of Biblical kingdom culture. We long for a total eradication of any cultural mind-sets or actions that come from anything but Jesus and His teachings. We need a mind and life change.

Our prayer is that through this first volume of *Culture of Revival*, you have been inspired by each chapter to now put into practice what has been received in faith.

Dream about a global church clothed in perseverance with joy. This was the prayer of Paul in Colossians 1:11 and the testimony of Jesus all the way to the cross. Great rewards await those who overcome and persevere in Christ for His kingdom. Let the phrase—perseverance with joy—and its truth forever mark you and your generation.

ABOUT THE AUTHOR: Sean Feucht is a husband, father, lover, fighter, optimist, musician, speaker, writer, revivalist, and founder of a grassroots global worship, prayer, and missions organization called Burn 24/7. His lifelong quest and dream is to witness a generation of burning hearts arise across the nations of the world with renewed faith, vision, and sacrificial pursuit after the Presence of God with reckless abandon. He has produced, recorded, and released twelve worship albums, numerous teaching resources, and recently coauthored his first book *Fire and Fragrance*. He is married to his gorgeous wife, Kate, and is a new father to their baby girl, Keturah Liv. He currently resides in Harrisburg, Pennsylvania (when he is not on planes, trains, or automobiles). Contact Sean at www.seanfeucht.com and www.burn24-7.com.

Endnotes

1   Ludwig, Charles. *Francis Asbury: God's Circuit Rider.* ©1984 by Mott Media, Inc., Publishers.

2   By permission. From Merriam-Webster's Collegiate Dictionary, 11th Edition. ©2012 by Merriam-Webster, Incorporated (www.merriam-webster.com).

3   Ibid.

4   http://www.gallup.com/poll/118399/More-Americans-Pro-Life-Than-Pro-Choice-First-Time.aspx. Copyright © 2012 Gallup, Inc. All rights reserved. Results are based on telephone interviews with 1,015 national adults, aged 18 and older, conducted May 7-10, 2009. For results based on the total sample of national adults, one can say with 95% confidence that the maximum margin of sampling error is ±3 percentage points.

5   Finley, James Bradley. *Autobiography of Rev. James B. Finley or, Pioneer Life in the West.* Cincinnati: Cranston and Curts; New York: Hunt and Eaton. Facsimile by Applewood Books, Bedford, Massachusetts. Originally published in 1853.

6   Stevens, Abel, LL.D., *History of the Methodist Episcopal Church of the United States of America. Volume II. The Planting and Training of American Methodism.* New York: Carlton & Porter, 1864. Page 234.

Authored by
Sean Feucht & Andy Byrd

Available in the Store at
www.seanfeucht.com

www.fireandfragrance.com

www.thecircuitrider.com

www.burn24-7.com